Douglas Emory Wilson
Anniston, Alabama
April 1994

Norma Aubertin-Potter
Kidlington, England
1st May 2008

THE BIOGRAPHER'S ART

THE BIOGRAPHER'S ART

New Essays

Edited by

JEFFREY MEYERS

Professor of English
University of Colorado

NEW AMSTERDAM
New York

Editorial matter, introduction and chapter 6 © Jeffrey Meyers 1989; chapter 1 © Donald
Greene 1989; chapter 2 © Maximillian E. Novak 1989; chapter 3 © Millicent Bell 1989;
chapter 4 © A. O. J. Cockshut 1989; chapter 5 © Phillip F. Herring 1989; chapter 7 ©
Eugene Goodheart 1989

First published in the United States of America in 1989 by
NEW AMSTERDAM BOOKS
of New York, Inc.
171 Madison Avenue
New York, NY 10016

by arrangement with The Macmillan Press Ltd.

ISBN 0–941533–52–2

For Frederick Crews

Contents

Notes on the Contributors

Millicent Bell is Professor of English at Boston University. She has written numerous articles on English and American literature and is the author of *Hawthorne's View of the Artist* (1962), *Edith Wharton and Henry James* (1965), *Marquand: An American Life* (1979), and editor of the Library of America, *Complete Novels of Nathaniel Hawthorne* (1983).

A. O. J. Cockshut is G. M. Young Lecturer in Nineteenth-Century Literature and Fellow of Hertford College, Oxford University. He is the author of *Anthony Trollope* (1955), *Anglican Attitudes* (1959), *The Imagination of Charles Dickens* (1961), *The Unbelievers* (1964), *Religious Controversies in the Nineteenth Century* (1966), *Truth to Life* (1974), *Man and Woman* (1977), *The Novel to 1900* (1980) and *The Art of Autobiography in 19th and 20th Century England* (1984).

Eugene Goodheart is the Edytha Macy Gross Professor of Humanities at Brandeis University. He is the author of *The Utopian Vision of D. H. Lawrence* (1963), *The Cult of the Ego: The Self in Modern Literature* (1968), *Culture and the Radical Conscience* (1973), *The Failure of Criticism* (1978), *The Skeptic Disposition in Contemporary Criticism* (1984) and *Pieces of Resistance* (1988).

Donald Greene is Leo S. Bing Professor emeritus of English, University of Southern California. Among his publications are *The Politics of Samuel Johnson* (1960), *The Age of Exuberance: Backgrounds to Eighteenth-Century Literature* (1970), *Samuel Johnson* ("Twayne's English Authors," 1970), and editions of *Samuel Johnson: A Collection of Critical Essays* (1965), Samuel Johnson, *Political Writings* (1977), *Samuel Johnson* (an anthology of his writings, "The Oxford Authors," 1984). He has also published extensively on Jane Austen and Evelyn Waugh.

Phillip F. Herring has taught at the University of Virginia, and has been a Visiting Fellow of Clare Hall, Cambridge University, and Visiting Professor at the University of New Mexico, the University of Oregon and Justus-Liebig Universität in Giessen, West Germany. He is now Professor of English at the University of Wisconsin, Madison, where he has taught since 1970. His publications include *Joyce's Uncertainty Principle* (1987) and editions of *Joyce's ULYSSES Notesheets in the British Museum* (1972) and *Joyce's Notes and Early Drafts for ULYSSES: Selections from the Buffalo Collection* (1977).

Jeffrey Meyers, Professor of English at the University of Colorado, is the author of several works on T. E. Lawrence and George Orwell; biographies of Katherine Mansfield (1978), Wyndham Lewis (1980) and Ernest Hemingway (1985); *Fiction and the Colonial Experience* (1973), *Painting and the Novel* (1975), *A Fever at the Core* (1976), *Married to Genius* (1977), *Homosexuality and Literature* (1977), *Hemingway: The Critical Heritage* (1982), *D. H. Lawrence and the Experience of Italy* (1982), *Disease and the Novel* (1985) and *Manic Power: Robert Lowell and His Circle* (1987). He has also edited *Wyndham Lewis: A Revaluation* (1980), *The Craft of Literary Biography* (1985), *D. H. Lawrence and Tradition* (1985) and *The Legacy of D. H. Lawrence* (1987).

Maximillian E. Novak is Professor of English at UCLA. He has written widely on eighteenth-century literature and is now writing a biography of Daniel Defoe. His works include *Economics and the Fiction of Daniel Defoe* (1962), *Defoe and the Nature of Man* (1963), *William Congreve* (1971), *Realism, Myth and History in Defoe's Fiction* (1983), *Eighteenth-Century English Literature* (1983) and volume XIII in *The California Edition of the Works of John Dryden* (1984).

Introduction

JEFFREY MEYERS

I

In *The Craft of Literary Biography*, which I edited for Macmillan in 1985, thirteen contemporary literary biographers considered, among other questions, how the biographer chooses a subject, uses biographical models, does archival research, conducts interviews, interprets evidence, establishes chronology, organizes material into a meaningful pattern and illuminates an author's work through a discussion of his life.

The Biographer's Art, a sequel to this book, is both a history of the genre and a substantial analysis of great biographies from the eighteenth century to the modern period. The seven distinguished life-writers and critics in this volume treat these biographies as works of art, consider the critical reception and discuss the qualities that characterize great works in this genre: original research that casts new light on the subject, a complete and accurate synthesis of both public and private life, an elegant yet lively style, a perceptive interpretation of character, a sound dramatic structure that brings the pattern of life into focus, an evocation of the cultural background and an insightful evaluation of the subject's achievement—the real justification of the work.

Michael Holroyd's response to the question of how far a biographer is prepared to go in order to get material illustrates the "constant struggle waged between a biographer and his subject, a struggle between the concealed self and the revealed self, the public self and the private."[1] Instead of laughing, as the questioner thought he might do, Holroyd—like the "publishing scoundrel" in James' "The Aspern Papers"— "became very serious and said that 'writing biography is

1

obsessional, and I'd be prepared to go to very, very great lengths indeed.' "[2]

The fear that the ruthless honesty of contemporary life-writing would "add a new terror to death"[3] has provoked authors as intensely private and public as Tennyson, James, Kipling, Roy Campbell and Nabokov (all subjects of biographies) to oppose the writing of biography. Tennyson felt that biographical exposure would leave its victims "ripped open like a pig."[4] As early as 1872 (when he was twenty-nine) James cautiously advocated a scorched earth policy that would destroy the biographer's sustenance: "Artists as time goes on will be likely to take the alarm, empty their table drawers and level the approaches to their privacy. The critics, psychologists and gossip-mongers [James lumped them all together] may then glean amid the stubble."[5] In his essay on George Sand (1897), James continued the military metaphor, emphasized the struggle and portrayed the artist fortified against the onslaughts of his pursuers: "The pale forewarned victim," he wrote, must fight back by destroying all evidence so that "with every track covered, every paper burnt and every letter unanswered, [he] will, in the tower of art, the invulnerable granite, stand, without a sally, the siege of all the years."[6] In a letter to James of 1908, the author of the recently published *Education of Henry Adams* metaphorically suggested that the "suicide" of autobiography was preferable to the "homicide" of biography: "This volume is a mere shield of protection in the grave. I advise you to take your own life in the same way, in order to prevent biographers from taking it in theirs."[7]

Kipling, punning on the term for biblical scholarship in the Victorian age, referred to biography as the "Higher Cannibalism."[8] And he concluded his thick volume of collected verse with the Jamesian appeal to his posthumous persecutors to concentrate on his works rather than his life:

> And for the little, little span
> The dead are borne in mind,
> Seek not to question other than
> The books I leave behind.[9]

After Kipling died, his daughter commissioned a biography by

Lord Birkenhead and then legally suppressed that work until after Birkenhead's death and her own.

In 1932, soon after the publication of Lytton Strachey's anti-heroic lives of eminent Elizabethans and Victorians, Roy Campbell, who was fond of heroic gestures in the battlefield and bullring, attacked Strachey's sneering and prurient attempts to denigrate the achievements of distinguished men: "Mr. Strachey's is often the 'breathless detachment' of a servant girl at a keyhole. . . . Since Mr. Strachey, by far the best of them, first patented his cheap, ready-made shot-gun for the hunting down of the 'great,' an epidemic of biographers has broken out. They have armed themselves with the same facile weapon and made war against every figure in history or literature who could possibly be suspected of having been privileged above the average."[10]

Nabokov, who carefully cultivated his public image in his autobiography and many interviews, called biography "psychoplagiarism" and satirized it in two of his novels. In the autobiographical *Real Life of Sebastian Knight* (1941), a half-brother of the late eponymous hero investigates his life and plans to write his biography. In the course of his research, Knight's half-brother condemns the greedy hack-work of his benighted predecessor, Mr. Goodman: "It is one thing to be an author's secretary, it is quite another to set down an author's life; and if such a task is prompted by the desire to get one's book into the market while the flowers on a fresh grave may still be watered with profit, it is still another matter to try to combine commercial haste with exhaustive research, fairness and wisdom."[11] And in *Look at the Harlequins!*, the anti-Freudian Nabokov denied that the psychoanalytic biographer could discover objective truth: "Reality would only be adulterated if I now started to narrate what you know, what I know, what nobody else knows, what shall never, never be ferreted out by a matter-of-fact, father of muck, mucking biographitist."[12]

Other novelists have also used fiction to express their anxiety about predatory biographers. In Henry James' "The Right Real Thing" (1900) an author's ghost prevents a scholar from writing his biography. In Elizabeth Taylor's "The Sisters" (1972), which seems to have been inspired by the life of Katherine Mansfield, a tactless biographer disturbs the placid existence of the conventional sister of a deceased writer. William

Golding's *The Paper Men* (1984) satirizes the crude machinations of an American biographer who harasses and victimizes a living writer. And Mark Harris' *Saul Bellow: Drumlin Woodchuck* (1980) describes, with astonishing naiveté, his own inept, ludicrous and humiliating attempts to gather information for a life of Saul Bellow.

Philip Larkin—an intensely private man who claimed that he had retreated to distant Hull to escape his would-be biographers—synthesized the subject's opposition to biography as well as the life-writer's resentment of his subject in his witty and ironic poem, "Posterity":

> Jake Balokowsky, my biographer,
> Has this page microfilmed. Sitting inside
> His air-conditioned cell at Kennedy
> In jeans and sneakers, he's no call to hide
> Some slight impatience with his destiny:
> "I'm stuck with this old fart at least a year."[13]

Despite this formidable opposition, a number of distinguished authors—Emerson, Froude, Yeats, Eliot and Auden—have actually encouraged life-writing. In "History," Emerson seemed to sabotage his ostensible subject with the famous pronouncement: "There is properly no history, only biography."[14] And Yeats, in characteristically fuzzy fashion, agreed that "nothing exists but a stream of souls, that all knowledge is biography."[15]

In his Preface to the *Life of Carlyle* (1882), J. A. Froude evoked the classical principles of Plutarch and Suetonius, and noted the moral benefits of subjecting the character and conduct of great men to close scrutiny: "When a man has exercised a large influence on the minds of his contemporaries, the world requires to know whether his own actions have corresponded with his teaching, and whether his moral and personal character entitles him to confidence. This is not idle curiosity, it is a legitimate demand. In proportion to a man's greatness is the scrutiny to which his conduct is submitted. . . . The publicity of private lives has been, is, and will be, either the reward or the penalty of intellectual distinction."

Eliot and Auden, who in their wills stipulated that no biography be written about them (Eliot's widow has so far prevented the publication of his letters as well as of an authorized life), have both, contrary to popular belief, advocated the advantages of biography. In a late essay, "The Frontiers of Criticism" (1956), Eliot saw no impediment to biography, rather blandly mentioned the requisite qualities of a life-writer and averred that the poet's life could illuminate his work: "Nor is there any reason why biographies of poets should not be written. Furthermore, the biographer of an author should possess some critical ability; he should be a man of taste and judgment, appreciative of the work of the man whose biography he undertakes. And on the other hand any critic seriously concerned with a man's work should be expected to know something about the man's life."[16]

In an early poem, "Who's Who," Auden dismissively wrote: "A shilling life will give you all the facts."[17] But in *Letters From Iceland* (1937), he approved without identifying the quatrain of Edmund Clerihew Bentley:

> Biography
> Is better than Geography,
> Geography's about maps,
> Biography's about chaps.[18]

Stephen Spender recorded that in later life Auden unequivocally stated that "Americans in their approach to biography demanded, and were right to demand, to know exactly what happened in people's lives."[19]

Napoleon once said that no one is a hero to his valet; to which Hegel retorted this was because valets were valets, not because heroes were not heroic. Hegel's point was that the great biographer must approach, if not equal, the intelligence, perception and style of his subject. Donald Greene has listed the essential qualities of a biography: exhaustive research, sceptical evaluation of evidence, scrupulous honesty, clarity and coherence, discriminating selectivity and sympathetic attraction to the subject.[20] In his *Paris Review* interview on "The Art of Biography," Leon Edel added that a biographer must be like a dog, always following a scent, and must be willing to engage in informed speculation: "The secret of biography resides in finding the link between talent and achievement. . . . [A biographer] defines the subject's nature by looking at what the mind brings to the surface and transforms into language."[21]

Edel has recently noted: "There exists, I am sorry to say, no criticism of biography worthy of the name. Reviewers and critics have learned how to judge plays, poems, novels—but they reveal their helplessness in the face of a biography."[22] *The Biographer's Art*, by concentrating on the aesthetics of the genre, responds to the need for serious criticism of life-writing.

II

The seven literary biographies considered in this book range from Johnson's *Life of Richard Savage* (1744) and Boswell's *Life of Johnson* (1791) through Strachey's *Eminent Victorians* (1918) and Symons' *The Quest for Corvo* (1934) to the three greatest biographies of the mid-twentieth century: Ellmann's *James Joyce* (1959), Painter's *Marcel Proust* (1959, 1965) and Edel's monumental *Henry James* (1953–72).[23]

Donald Greene—who is now completing the late James Clifford's biography with a volume on the last two decades of Johnson's life—offers a characteristically lively and learned account of Johnson's most significant biographical work. He first surveys Johnson's shorter biographical writings, especially *The Lives of the Poets*, praises "his shrewd psychological comments on the motivation of his subjects and those they interacted with," and argues that "it is Johnson's theory of biography [especially in *Rambler*, No. 60] rather than his practice that entitles him to praise." Greene discusses the ambiguous facts of Savage's life, "one of the great *causes célèbres* of the period," as well as Johnson's use of printed sources, his fascination with the character of Savage (whom he knew personally) and his ambivalent attitude toward Savage's behavior. Greene shows that Johnson's treatment of the persecution of the hero by his fiendish mother, the villainous Lady Macclesfield, "sounds like a fantasized version of Mrs. Michael Johnson of Lichfield, [and] Richard Savage often sounds like young Sam."

Maximillian Novak—who is currently writing the life of Daniel Defoe—begins his authoritative chapter on the *Life of Johnson* by considering Germaine Greer's objections to biography and Macaulay's condemnation of Boswell. Novak discusses the influence of Rousseau on Boswell's sensibility, Boswell's odd combination of egotism and depression, his portrayal of Johnson in *Journal of a Tour to the Hebrides*, and the personal relationship of Johnson and Boswell. Johnson saw Boswell—who considered himself a disciple and surrogate son—as "the living exemplar of the kind of biographer he would have wanted . . . devoted to telling the truth and to finding the truth" in minute particulars and characteristic conversation. Novak notes Boswell's skill as a narrator, his ability to raise "the kind of question that drew out the best in Johnson's thinking" and the rich dramatic tension of his staged scenes, and offers an acute analysis of the encounter between Johnson and John Wilkes. He relates Boswell's method to the realistic fiction of Defoe and Richardson, and praises his ability to probe deeply into Johnson's feelings and motives.

Millicent Bell—who has published a biography of John Marquand and is now writing a life of Henry James—argues that "what sent shock waves through the first readers [of *Eminent Victorians*] was the bold assumption of an attitude which did not predicate veneration or even respect for its human subjects," for Strachey had no allegiance or obligations to the figures he portrayed. Bell is particularly illuminating about how Strachey used his abundant sources: how he adopted their facts and interpretations while introducing a parodistic element, how he shifted the emphasis—through symbolic details—from pious hagiography to irreverent sarcasm. Bell comments on his haphazard vision and flagrant lack of seriousness, his sense of form and dramatic coherence, his idea of history and historical probability: "[he] never looked at a document; he had only his [sound] intuitions." She concludes that the theme of the book is "not so much the effect of religion on the Victorian personality . . . [but of] creatures possessed of a personal energy that had nothing particularly religious about it."[24]

A. O. J. Cockshut—who has written perceptively on Victorian biography and modern autobiography—considers Symons' life of the strange and solitary Frederick Rolfe, a "fantasist of egoism" who combined Savage's mercenary ingratitude with Strachey's precious perversity. Cockshut defines Rolfe as a cult figure and dandy. He describes Symons' character, taste, method, informants and accuracy, his attraction to—and similarity to—his subject ("a biographer should choose his subject as a dandy chooses his suit"), and places the

innovative "autobiography of a biographer" in the context of
Victorian and modern life-writing. He comments on Symons'
investigations of Rolfe's inversion, paranoia and religious quest:
"Church matters were mostly a matter of millinery to him," a
friend observed. "The form of [Symons'] book," Cockshut
writes, "tends to assimilate his quest to a detective's search for
truth in a 'mystery thriller.'" His somewhat severe verdict is that
Symons "is very good at discovering things, very open-minded
in accepting evidence that seems to point in different directions,
but in the end he just fails to focus his subject," to explain his
complex character and bizarre behavior.

Phillip Herring—who has done valuable work on Joyce's
manuscripts—discusses Herbert Gorman's early life of Joyce
and Ellmann's theory of biography: his belief in "biographical
license," speculation in the absence of factual evidence.
Focusing on a single representative chapter of *James Joyce*,
Herring examines Ellmann's portrayal of Joyce's self-indulgent
character, his relations with his brother Stanislaus and the
major theme of genius triumphing over adversity. Herring
surveys the critical response to the biography and the charges
(especially in the harsh review by Ellmann's great rival in Joyce
studies, Hugh Kenner) that Ellmann relied too heavily
on Stanislaus, was sometimes inaccurate, used fiction for
biographical evidence, and employed an ironic and
unsympathetic tone. Herring evaluates, in the light of recent
scholarship, Ellmann's treatment of Joyce's religious faith and
commitment to Socialist politics, the new material in the revised
edition of the biography, Ellmann's editing of the Joyce letters,
and the controversial inclusion of the obscene correspondence
with his wife Nora in the *Selected Letters* of 1975. After noting
Ellmann's limitations, Herring commends the eloquence and
narrative power of the "brilliant, witty, humane biographer."

The chapter on Painter's *Marcel Proust* by Jeffrey Meyers—
the author of biographies of Katherine Mansfield, Wyndham
Lewis and Ernest Hemingway—is based on extensive
correspondence with George Painter, who writes: "My subject
has fed upon me. He's taken my life blood while I've tried to
give him life." Meyers begins with a brief biography of Painter:
his training in Classics, his breadth of learning, his work habits,
his attraction to Proust and his "attempts to probe the mystery
of artistic creation." He describes Painter's biographical models

and principles, and explains why he deliberately avoided anyone who had ever known Proust and worked entirely from primary sources. He analyzes Painter's dogmatic Preface to *Marcel Proust*, which "recklessly abandons the scholar's false humility and debt to his predecessors," and his desire to connect every aspect of Proust's "creative autobiography" to factual reality. After a discussion of the enthusiastic and vituperative critical response to the biography, Meyers considers Painter's treatment of Proust's social background, complex motives, relations with parents and sexual life, and concludes that Painter "triumphantly fulfills what he believes to be the author's highest purpose: to communicate 'the state of vision in which the book was written so that the writer's revelation becomes the reader's.' "

Eugene Goodheart examines the idea in James' own autobiographies that the "truth" of the past was available only through creative memory and Edel's belief that the biographer–subject relationship is antagonistic. He states that Edel successfully finds a middle ground which enables him to uncover the "secrets" of James' life and, at the same time, to preserve empathy with his subject. Goodheart shows how Edel's "antiseptic" psychoanalytic bias and impressive intuitions influence his portrayal of James' "Vastation" and "obscure hurt," his relations with his brother William, his erotic incapacity, his problematic attitude to "sacred" women who served his spiritual needs, and his intense feelings for the young sculptor, Hendrik Anderson. Goodheart also analyzes the essence of Edel's art and themes: his sense of time and deliberate retardation of narrative movement, the uneventful nature of James' external life and progress of his consciousness as well as the "erotics of landscapes" in James' imagination, the Anglicization "that provided a standard for cross-cultural judgments," the inordinate price of art and the renunciation of ordinary life.

The masterful biographies by Ellmann, Painter and Edel, who continue the tradition begun by Johnson and Boswell and show the influence of Strachey's innovative work, confirm that biography is now "the most living art form." By firing the facts of an author's life by their own imagination and illuminating the relationship between daily existence and imaginative life, these life-writers follow the same process as fiction writers and create their own significant works of art.

CHAPTER ONE

Samuel Johnson's *The Life of Richard Savage*

DONALD GREENE

A wicked, heartless and unscrupulous woman, a Countess no less, grows weary of her uneasy marriage to a high-ranking English Earl. She gives birth to a son fathered by her paramour, another Earl, and makes a public confession of adultery as the most obvious and expeditious method of obtaining her liberty. The authorities comply, and a bill of divorcement is enacted, which incidentally illegitimates the son, who otherwise would be the legal heir to her husband's title and estate.

The inhuman mother is not merely indifferent to her by-blow; she hates and incessantly persecutes him. When his natural father is on his deathbed and concerned to make provision for him, she lies to him and tells him that the child is dead, so that the six thousand pounds he had planned to leave him is bestowed elsewhere. The boy's grandmother takes pity on him and arranges for his early schooling (in which he distinguishes himself by his genius and industry). His hateful mother, however, forms schemes, fortunately frustrated, to have him kidnapped and sold as an indentured servant (virtually a slave) to the American plantations, or to have him apprenticed to a shoemaker so as to ensure his social obscurity.

The boy rises above all this. While still in his teens, he writes poems and plays that win him the esteem of the London literary world. He comes upon letters from his grandmother that reveal to him his true identity. Anxious to gain some affection from his cruel mother, he often paces, in the dark evenings, for several hours before her door, in hopes of seeing her as she might come by accident to the window, or cross her apartment with a candle in her hand. Once he ventures to enter her house,

11

finding its door by accident open, and approaches her, hoping she may take pity on him. When she sees him, she screams and orders her servants to eject him. Worst comes to worst when, after he had been unjustly convicted of murder in a tavern brawl and sentenced to death, and pleas are made to the king and queen for a pardon for him (one is eventually granted), her malice is so great that she argues against such clemency to one who has made an attempt on her life.

He never approaches her again. For the remaining twenty or so years of his life, he pursues a career as a writer, usually in wretched poverty, never quite realizing the potential his friends see in him, and often touchily quarreling with those who try to befriend him. These failings can be accounted for and condoned by the terrible trauma of his early life. He dies, in his forties, in a debtors' prison in Bristol, his malevolent mother, who had shortened his life by her maternal offices, outliving him by a decade.

Such, in brief, is the narrative of Samuel Johnson's *Account of the Life of Mr. Richard Savage, Son of the Earl Rivers*. Many of the expressions used here, including such words as "wicked," "cruel," "inhuman," "malice," and "shortened," are quoted directly from Johnson. Whatever else may be said about the piece, it is a good read—indeed, a real tearjerker.

"To write the life of him who excelled all mankind in writing the lives of others . . . is an arduous, and may be reckoned in me a presumptuous task." So James Boswell begins his *Life of Johnson*. As well as being a tremendous compliment to his subject, it is also, in spite of its seeming self-depreciation, an advertisement for himself—like Norman Mailer after him, Boswell was no mean adept at this exercise—and he immediately follows it up with a vicious denigration of his two chief competitors as biographers of Johnson, Sir John Hawkins and Hester (Thrale) Piozzi. Posterity has embraced—perhaps because it is so easy to remember—Macaulay's verdict that Boswell's *Life* is the world's greatest biography, as pre-eminent in that class as Homer's epics and Shakespeare's dramas in theirs, and has on the whole paid little attention to Boswell's tribute to *il miglior fabbro*. There have been studies of Johnson's biographical *oeuvre*, but no one, I think, has ever attempted a serious assessment of it in relation to the enormous, nearly two-millennia output of biography that preceded him, from Suetonius, Diogenes Laertius and Plutarch, up through Vasari to Conyers Middleton's controversial *Cicero*, published only three years before Johnson's *Savage*—not to mention great autobiographies, such as Cellini's and Clarendon's.

Perhaps Johnson himself would not have made the claim that Boswell makes for him. But there is no question that he is an important figure in the history of life-writing (the word "biography" seems to have been introduced into English by Dryden in the preface to his translation of Plutarch, 1683), both as practitioner and theorist. The 522 pages of J. D. Fleeman's collection of Johnson's *Early Biographical Writings*[1] contain thirty items, ranging in date from 1738 to 1769. Many are short pieces concerning individuals in the news at the time, some of them extended obituaries such as those of the Continental scholars Pieter Burman and the young prodigy Jean-Philippe Barretier, published in the *Gentleman's Magazine* and other periodicals with which Johnson was connected (the advent of such literary journals in the eighteenth century as vehicles for serious biography ought to be noted), some longish prefaces to editions of the subject's works, like those of Roger Ascham, the Renaissance scholar and teacher, and Sir Thomas Browne. They have been unjustly neglected. Although the factual information in them comes, as is the case with most modern biography, from earlier printed sources, Johnson can never resist interspersing it with his own inferences and judgments on the events recorded, and shrewd and thought-provoking interpolations they usually are. Notable among them are the lives of Herman Boerhaave, the greatest scientist of the time, whose advanced, empiricist approach to science Johnson applauds; Frederick, King of Prussia (later termed "the Great"), then at the height of his early career as a warrior; Sir Francis Drake, a long (nearly 25,000 words), lively, highly readable account, thoughtfully and critically compiled from several contemporary sources, chiefly of the earlier life of the great naval commander and explorer, culminating in a finely-told narrative of his circumnavigation of the world.[2]

Boswell's compliment to Johnson as biographer probably derives from his fame (or notoriety, for some of Johnson's judgments in it aroused great antagonism) as the author of what Boswell and his successors thought of as *The Lives of the Poets*. It is well to stress that this is a misnomer, and that the work was not conceived of as biography pure and simple. What happened was this. In 1777, a group of London publishers, fearing that the tenuous claim they maintained to copyright in English poetry from Milton onward was about to be infringed by an Edinburgh firm, decided to try to bolster it by bringing out a multi-volumed anthology of that poetry—in the end, it comprised fifty-two writers—and, as publishers still do, cast around for some celebrity to compose short prefaces to the works of each author, in the hope of increasing the sales of material that had long been in print. The obvious first choice was Johnson, then in his late sixties, who, no doubt to their delight, accepted the commission for a mere 200 guineas (which averages out to around 4 guineas—present equivalent perhaps £80 or $120—per preface).

A modern scholar—rightly, I think—makes the distinction between "pure biography"—"the record of a living being . . . written for itself, for its own intrinsic interest"—and "the prefatory life, [which] owed its existence merely to the need to give some sort of authority to the works it preceded."[3] Johnson probably had no illusions about the majority of the short prefaces he turned out for the host of mediocre poets in the collection—always the great majority in a group of fifty selected from any century—belonging to the latter rather than the former class. *The Lives of the Poets* was not Johnson's title for the compilation. Its first edition bore the title *Prefaces, Biographical and Critical, to the Works of the English Poets*. When a second edition was proposed, Johnson suggested either "An Account of the Lives and Works of Some of the Most Eminent English Poets" or "The English Poets Biographically and Critically Considered."[4] He certainly did not want the fact overlooked that an important part of what he had written was critical rather than biographical. But "The Lives of" was a time-honored and popular designation. A Dublin edition in 1779 used the title *The Lives of the English Poets; and a Criticism on Their Works*, and the London second edition chose *The Lives of the Most Eminent English Poets* (large type); *with Critical Observations on Their Works* (smaller type); and before long title-pages of reprints were omitting the "critical observations" and even the "English."

The prefaces vary greatly in length. Thirty-six of the fifty-two (nearly three-fourths) run from 4 to 39 paragraphs, with a median of 19, averaging around 125 words per paragraph. This no doubt was about what Johnson's publishers expected for their 200 guineas; but it can hardly be maintained that a group of prefatory notes of this exiguous size, a substantial part of each occupied with critical observations rather than accounts of the subject's life, is a major contribution to biography. Eight others range between 40 and 80 paragraphs. Assuming that two-thirds of each preface is biographical rather than critical— a generous estimate—we have here biographical sketches of from 4,000 to 8,000 words each. And, of course, as in his earlier biographical work, the great majority of Johnson's information comes from earlier published material. Johnson is perfectly frank about this; no need for him to make a secret of it, any more than there would be for the author of a modern ten- to twenty-page preface to an anthology of Milton, Pope, Swift or Eliot.[5]

Whatever claim based on the *Prefaces* Johnson may have to Boswell's accolade for pre-eminence in biography must come from the eight longest of them (seven if we omit the reprint of the 1744 *Savage*), running from 141 paragraphs (*Swift*) to 384 (*Pope*), again with sizable portions of them devoted to criticism (indeed most of *Cowley* is critical, Cowley's name having raised the whole subject of "metaphysical" poetry). It was this unexpected bounty that impelled Johnson's publishers to present him with an extra hundred guineas. It also perhaps complicated their publishing plans, since prefixing a 45,000-word essay to their selection from Pope's poetry and perfunctory notes of fewer than 1,000 words to those from Hammond, Somerville, Duke, Pomfret and Stepney might have looked odd. They got round this by dropping Johnson's "prefaces" as prefaces to individual selections, and printing them together in separate volumes—an action that obscured their original purpose. But even in the longest of the "lives" Johnson contributed little in the way of original research—though he did contribute some[6]— but took most of his biographical data from such earlier and more detailed works as Ruffhead and Spence on Pope, Orrery, Hawkesworth and Deane Swift on Swift, Tickell on Addison. The excellence of the biographical parts of Johnson's prefaces is in his shrewd psychological comments on the motivation of his subjects and those they interacted with.

A much more plausible thesis is that it is Johnson's theory of biography rather than his practice that entitles him to praise. The heart of that theory is his great opening sentence of *Rambler* No. 60, which is a sound basis for criticism not only of biography but of imaginative literature of any kind:

> All joy or sorrow for the happiness or calamities of others is produced by an act of the imagination that realizes [makes real] the event, however fictitious, or approximates it [brings it near], however remote, by placing us, for a time, in the condition of him whose fortune we contemplate; so that we feel, while the deception lasts [while "the willing suspension of disbelief for a time," as Coleridge was later to put it, endures] whatever motions [emotions] would be excited by the same good or evil happening to ourselves.

He goes on to argue that great military or political leaders, whose names have become famous in history, are not the best subjects for biography, since it is difficult for the ordinary reader to "identify" or empathize with them. Rather, biography should be concerned with those with whom the ordinary reader *can* identify. "I have often thought," he writes, "that there has rarely passed a life of which a judicious and faithful narrative would not be useful. . . . We are all prompted by the same motives, all deceived by the same fallacies, all animated by hope, obstructed by dangers, entangled by desire, and seduced by pleasure. . . . The scholar who passed his life among his books, the merchant who conducted only his own affairs, the priest whose sphere of action was not extended beyond his duty" are at least as worthy of the biographer's attention as a Julius Caesar or Alexander the Great. And, for the same reason, it is not the public triumphs of the military or political hero that the biographer should chiefly be concerned with, but the seemingly minor, even if "undignified," details of private life: rather to tell "not how any man became great, but how he was made happy; not how he lost the favour of his prince, but how he became discontented with himself."[7]

This is a resounding manifesto for what later came to be called "psychological biography," an anticipation of Lytton Strachey's "Human beings are too important to be treated as mere symptoms of the past. They have a value which . . . is eternal, and must be felt for its own sake."[8] To be sure, it may not have been as revolutionary a doctrine as has sometimes been asserted. Even Plutarch, who insisted on the didactic purpose of biography, to provide examples of good lives to be followed and bad ones to be avoided (if necessary, suppressing minor peccadilloes of "the good," so as to make them better "role models"), enjoyed, as his translator Dryden noted, and let his readers enjoy, small and seemingly trivial details in the lives of his subjects. Astonishingly, Roger North, in a manuscript preface, not published until the late twentieth century, to his biographies of his brothers (one a lawyer, one a merchant, one a scholar), had earlier, and forcefully, put forward every one of Johnson's theses.[9] Yet a doubt persists: how confident can we be of the ability of even such shrewd students of humanity as Johnson and Freud to ascertain the real causes of happiness or discontent in specific human beings?

The biographical work of Johnson's that most fully exemplifies his theory is *An Account of the Life of Mr. Richard Savage, Son of the Earl Rivers*, published in 1744, when Johnson was in his thirties and a struggling, unknown staff writer for the *Gentleman's Magazine* (the work, like the great majority of Johnson's, was published anonymously). It is perhaps entitled to be called his only full-length biography—some 42,500 words, compared with its closest competitor, the biographical part of the preface to Pope, around 30,000. Moreover, unlike the *Pope*, much of it, though, unfortunately, not all, is based on first-hand knowledge of his subject.

Its origin was one of the great *causes célèbres* of the period. In 1683, Charles Gerard, Viscount Brandon, son and heir of the first Earl of Macclesfield, who had been a distinguished military commander on the royalist side in the Civil War and was later a sturdy opponent of James II and supporter of William III, married Anne Mason, the fifteen-year-old daughter of a Cheshire squire. Brandon was twenty-four. After a year and a half, the young couple separated. According to Clarence Tracy (whose biography of Richard Savage is, by modern standards of careful research and factual accuracy, far superior to Johnson's), they

> quarreled over money, found fault with each other's relations, bickered over the use of the one family coach, and resorted to all the petty methods married people have of making each

other miserable. . . . Her maid declared before the House of Lords that Lord Brandon refused to sleep with his wife after the first week or two.

Brandon's record was that of "a man of violent and criminal character. A short time before his marriage, while on a drunken orgy, he murdered an innocent boy in the London streets. Less than a month after his wedding he was arrested and confined to the Tower of London for four months on a charge of treason."[10]

Anne's father-in-law, the old Earl, evicted her from the Gerard house in London (he was to die in 1694, whereupon Lord and Lady Brandon became Earl and Countess of Macclesfield) and for the next fifteen years she lived with her sister Lady Brownlow. When she was in her mid-twenties, she fell in the way of Richard Savage, Earl Rivers, a handsome man in his thirties, a successful soldier and politician, and a notorious rake, already with a progeny of illegitimate children. In 1695, Anne gave birth to a daughter by him, and in 1697 a son.

It was in that year that Lord Macclesfield began proceedings for divorce against the wife from whom he had been separated for so long. Presumably the cause was the birth of the son, who, if action were not taken, would be the legal heir to his title and estate. The proceedings began in the ecclesiastical courts, which had the power to grant a legal separation—a decree of divorce *a mensa et thoro*—but nothing more. Before the case had been decided, however, Macclesfield shifted the proceedings to Parliament, which alone had the power to pass an act granting a dissolution *a vinculo matrimonii*—a cancellation of the marriage bond—permitting the parties legally to remarry. This may not have been Macclesfield's motive; he died four years later, never having remarried. The former Lady Macclesfield, however, in 1700 married Colonel Henry Brett, a friend of Addison's, living with him quietly, and, so far as is known, happily, until his death in 1724, and herself living until the age of eighty-five, dying in 1753.

Only five such pieces of legislation were passed by Parliament before 1714, and this one produced much heated debate in the House of Lords. Among the arguments put forward on behalf of Lady Macclesfield, who protested her essential innocence and even victimization in the matter, was that Macclesfield and

Rivers were in collusion so that she could be found guilty of adultery. But in the end the action had the consequences probably desired by both parties: Lord Macclesfield succeeded in having both Lady Macclesfield's children by Rivers declared illegitimate,[11] and Lady Macclesfield had restored to her the financial settlement paid to Macclesfield at the time of their marriage.

The scandal eventually died down. But in 1712 its memory was revived when the great Duke of Hamilton and Lord Mohun, both related to Macclesfield by marriage, killed each other in a duel over the provisions of his will. (Readers of Thackeray's *Henry Esmond* will remember the incident vividly.) It was again revived when, in 1716, General George MacCartney, who had been Mohun's second and fled to France after the duel, was brought to trial on the charge of having been an accessory to, if not a principal in, the murder of Hamilton. It was about then that a hitherto unknown young man "appeared out of nowhere" (as Tracy puts it), and, answering to a well substantiated charge of publishing seditious Jacobite propaganda (it was the time of the Jacobite uprising of 1715), gave his name as "Mr. Savage, natural son to the late Earl Rivers."

History is full of impostors who maintained that they were children of famous individuals, children who had been thought to have perished in youth, but who had miraculously survived. In the fifteenth century, Perkin Warbeck and Lambert Simnel laid claim to the throne of England, one alleging that he was Edward IV's son, the Duke of York, supposedly put to death in the Tower by Richard III, the other that he was the son of Edward's brother, the Duke of Clarence. Both were accepted as her nephews by Edward's sister, the Duchess of Burgundy, glad to make political capital of the disturbances in England caused by them. Some twenty-seven different claimants maintained that they were the Dauphin, Louis XVII, who had died in prison at the time of the execution of his parents Louis XVI and Marie Antoinette, the best known being the "King" in Mark Twain's *Huckleberry Finn*. Two young men calling themselves "Stuart" (their real name was Allen) find a niche in the *Dictionary of National Biography* through their claim that they were grandsons of the Young Pretender, and had a receptive audience in Victorian Britain. When the wealthy young Roger Tichbourne was reported drowned in 1854, his anguished

mother advertised throughout the world for news that he had
survived, and to her delight received a reply from an Australian
named Arthur Orton, who mastered Tichbourne's early history
well enough to convince the mother, but not enough to convince
an English court, which found him guilty of forgery and perjury.
It is only a short time since the death was reported of the
woman who insisted that she was Czar Nicholas II's daughter,
the Grand Duchess Anastasia, who had been miraculously
preserved in the massacre at Ekaterinburg, and succeeded in
convincing a great many people.

The story of the long-lost rightful son and heir, concealed
and persecuted by a wicked uncle or stepmother, is one of the
oldest and most popular themes of folk- and fairy-tale, and even
of later fiction, as in the Gothic novelists and Dickens. Indeed,
it is not uncommon for children dissatisfied with their actual
paternity to fantasize that they were fathered by someone more
glamorous. What happened to the child born to Lady
Macclesfield in 1697 is not known. A few days after his birth he
was christened as "Richard Smith," Smith being the name
Lady Macclesfield had temporarily assumed. His physical
father, Rivers, acted as godfather and gave the baby his
forename. He was then put out to nurse, as children of all but
the lowest classes then were (Johnson, for instance, was).
Burials are recorded of two children whose names, ages and
places of residence seem to have corresponded with those of the
child, one of them a Richard Smith, though with so common a
name, there is no assurance that this was Lady Macclesfield's
son. But given the rate of infant mortality at the time, an early
death is not improbable. The boy's sister Ann, two years older,
died in early childhood.

An even darker area of obscurity, apart from the spectacular
story he himself put forward, is the earlier history of the young
man who surfaced in 1715, calling himself "Richard Savage,
son of the Earl Rivers" (who had died in 1712). All the scanty
available evidence has been carefully scrutinized, especially by
Clarence Tracy, whose investigation is a model of meticulous
research. Professor Tracy's conclusion is that "the case against
the literal truth of his [Savage's] assertions has not been
proven." But it is notoriously difficult to prove a negative
proposition, and many would argue that the *onus probandi* rests
on those who put forward the affirmative one—that is, primarily,

"Savage" himself. One may agree with Professor Tracy that "such consistency and pertinacity as he displayed through twenty-eight years, to say nothing of his success in convincing almost all his contemporaries, would have been possible only to a scoundrel of genius or to a man who honestly and deeply believed in himself."[12] But the same could be affirmed of, say, the woman who maintained, consistently and pertinaciously, for at least an equal number of years, that she was the Grand Duchess Anastasia of Russia, who convinced perhaps an equal number of her contemporaries, and about whom as many novels, plays and "biographies" have been written as about "Savage." The dividing line between the individual who with psychopathic conviction "honestly believes" in a demonstrable lie about himself and the "scoundrel of genius" is not so clearly definable as Professor Tracy suggests. An example is the schizophrenic astronomer of the later chapters of *Rasselas*, who "honestly believes" that he controls the weather and the movements of the heavenly bodies. It required a long course of psychotherapy to disabuse him of this belief, and one wonders whether Johnson's encounters with Savage two decades earlier had not given him some insight into the problem.

At any rate, the young man who called himself Savage, once he had emerged from obscurity, quickly proved himself to be clever, plausible, ingratiating, fluent with his tongue and pen, even "charismatic" (or at least a highly successful manipulator of others)—and a perpetual trouble-maker. John Hawkins, with whom Johnson was intimate at the same time he was with Savage, thus described him, not without a hint of sarcasm:

> Savage, as to his exterior, was, to a remarkable degree, accomplished: he was a handsome, well-made man, and very courteous in the modes of salutation. I have been told that in taking off his hat and disposing it under his arm, and in his bow, he displayed as much grace as those actions were capable of.[13]

With the publication of "correct" if uninspired verses on such topical matters as the Bangorian controversy, he soon became known in the higher reaches of Grub Street, attracting and attaching himself to such people as Sir Richard Steele, the actor Robert Wilks, the actress Anne Oldfield, the novelist Eliza

Haywood, the wealthy dilettantish patron of literature Aaron Hill (with most of whom he quarreled sooner or later). His greatest success as a writer was a historical drama, *Sir Thomas Overbury*, given four performances at Drury Lane in 1723. He was an adept sponger, even at one time—before he turned against her publicly—extracting an allowance from his putative mother Mrs. Brett and her nephew the Earl of Tyrconnel (there is just a hint of possible threats of blackmail in the latter two cases of charity). When Colley Cibber—who was at least no worse a poet than Savage—was appointed Poet Laureate, the chagrined Savage announced that he was "volunteer laureate" to Queen Caroline (as an acquaintance said, he might as well have stated that he had become a volunteer lord), and the Queen granted him an annual pension of £50, the discontinuance of which, after her death, caused Savage great indignation.

Disaster nearly overtook him in November 1727. During an evening of drinking and making the rounds of the taverns, he and two friends, Gregory and Merchant, got into a drunken brawl with another group, in the midst of which Savage drew his sword and ran one of them, named Sinclair (who was unarmed), through his belly. Sinclair died the next morning, identifying Savage, who with his friends had tried to run off but was arrested, as his assailant. The next month Savage, Gregory and Merchant were tried for murder at the Old Bailey before the famous "hanging judge" Page and a jury. In spite of an unconvincing plea of self-defence or, alternatively, accident, Savage and Gregory were quickly convicted (Merchant, who was unarmed, was found guilty of manslaughter), and, in spite of an elegant speech by Savage pleading for clemency, he and Gregory were sentenced to be hanged. Savage's friends immediately rallied round and put together a 29-page pamphlet designed to convince the king and his advisers that Savage, because of his dreadful persecution by his mother, the former Lady Macclesfield, when he was young, and his exemplary behavior and demonstrated genius since that time, deserved to be pardoned. The effort succeeded; and with the publication of two best-selling self-pitying poems, *The Bastard*, denouncing his alleged mother, and *The Wanderer*, denouncing society for its neglect of genius like his, Savage entered what Johnson later called "the golden part of Mr. Savage's life."

Where was Samuel Johnson when the exciting events of 1727

took place in London? He was a teen-ager in provincial Lichfield, sulkily helping to mind his father's bookshop.[14] In 1728 an unexpected small legacy enabled him to attend Oxford for a little more than an academic year, not long enough for him to obtain a degree. This was followed by nearly a decade of wandering about the Midlands, doing a little writing and in unsuccessful pursuit of a career as a schoolteacher, until, in March 1737, accompanied by his former pupil David Garrick, he set out for London to try to make some kind of living as a Grub Street writer.

Just when he met Savage there is uncertain. In his first published work to win critical acclaim (it was praised by Pope), the poem *London* (May 1738), the spokesman, Thales, rants away in a vein not uncharacteristic of Savage about the degeneracy of politics and morals in contemporary London, and ends by retreating to the primitive simplicity of Wales. It has often been suggested that Johnson must have met Savage before this time, particularly since the previous month Johnson had printed in the *Gentleman's Magazine* a Latin distich in ecstatic praise of Savage, which may be translated "O thou, whose heart burns with devotion to the human race,/May the human race honour and cherish thee!" And of course Savage did go into exile in Wales, assisted by a subscription raised by his literary friends, who were anxious to get rid of him and remove him from the too powerful temptations of London (in his *Account* Johnson says movingly that he "parted from the author of this narrative with tears in his eyes"). But this did not take place until July 1739. Savage had been a good enough self-advertiser so that personal acquaintance with him was not necessary for him to be made the model for Thales.

At most, it seems as though Johnson can have known Savage personally for only a little more than a year. But Savage's "charisma" seems to have worked powerfully on the younger man. Like Johnson, he had been (he maintained) the victim of poverty and neglect, or worse than neglect, and both, at this time, were outspoken radicals and (as one psychiatrist puts it) "injustice collectors."[15] If, as Savage asserted, he was only eighteen when his first publications became known—though of course we have no real evidence of his age—he had hardly been neglected by the literary world of London; but poverty he certainly knew—when the frequent hand-outs from his friends were exhausted, as they quickly were. Hawkins reports: "They seemed both to agree in the vulgar opinion that the world is divided into two classes, of men of merit without riches, and men of wealth without merit."[16] Johnson told him and others of nights wandering with Savage around the squares of Westminster without even the few pennies needed for a bed in a squalid cellar—Savage was sometimes reduced to huddling on a heap of warm ashes outside a glass factory—denouncing the Walpole administration, which was bringing the country to ruin, "dethroning princes, establishing new forms of government, and giving laws to the several states of Europe."

Given Savage's ability to win over such far from naive individuals as Pope, Steele and Tyrconnel (an experienced politician), his effect on the young and idealistic Johnson, fresh from the backwoods, is not to be wondered at. But Johnson seems to have been more than ordinarily susceptible to the blandishments of the many confidence men who flourished in eighteenth-century Britain, notably the "Formosan" Psalmanazar and the Milton forger Lauder. Later, of course, he saw through "Ossian" Macpherson, and, like many others, through Chatterton. Yet he could not resist making an expedition to Bristol to see the chest where the Rowley poems had been "discovered," commenting, "This is the most extraordinary young man that has encountered my knowledge. It is wonderful how the whelp has written such things."[17] Mrs. Thrale remarked: "Dear Dr. Johnson was not difficult to be imposed on where the *Heart* came into question."[18]

The fascination Savage held for Johnson is reminiscent of that which the wild man Basil Seal—apparently based on one or two early acquaintances of his—had for Evelyn Waugh. Like Savage, obtaining friends and patrons, Basil "never had much difficulty getting jobs." Waugh writes: "The trouble had always been in keeping them, for he regarded a potential employer as his opponent in a game of skill. All Basil's resource and energy went into hoodwinking him into surrender; once he had received his confidence he lost interest."[19] As Johnson puts it: "It was his [Savage's] peculiar happiness that he scarcely ever found a stranger whom he did not leave a friend; but it must likewise be added that he had not often a friend long, without obliging him to become a stranger."[20] Among would-be benefactors whom Savage alienated were Steele, whose own follies Savage publicly

ridiculed, uncaring that his words would certainly be reported
to his patron; Tyrconnel—Savage would bring his tavern
companions to Tyrconnel's house and make them free of his
host's wine cellar, and, when Tyrconnel made him presents of
valuable books from his library, expensively bound and stamped
with Tyrconnel's arms, would sell them to booksellers, on
whose stalls Tyrconnel had the mortification of seeing them
displayed for sale; finally, the citizens of Bristol, where Savage
ended his life in a debtors' prison: a number of them had
furnished him with charity; he responded with a satiric poem
which heaped the utmost vilification on the inhabitants of
Bristol. Though, interestingly, the greatest of all his patrons,
Alexander Pope, himself from an oppressed, "minority"
background, never wavered in his compassion for him until
almost the very end.

After four unhappy years in Wales and Bristol, often trying
to find excuses to return to London and complaining about lack
of support from his friends there, Savage died in August 1743.
Johnson and his editor Cave immediately published, in the
Gentleman's Magazine for that month, an advertisement for a
forthcoming *Life of Savage*, "by a person who was favoured with
his confidence," which "may have a tendency to the preservation
of his memory from insults or calumnies" and will "gratify the
lovers of truth and wit" by giving them an account which will
not be "only a novel, filled with romantick adventures and
imaginary amours." This of course was to warn off anyone else
who might have a notion of profiting from the news of the
celebrity's death. Johnson finished it by December, when he
received fifteen guineas for it from Cave, and the 186-page book
was published in February 1744.

The work might be considered as roughly divided into two
parts, the opening one-third or so concentrating on the
persecution of the hero by his fiendish mother, and the
remainder dealing with Savage's later relationships with others,
some knowledge of which Johnson had at first hand. For the
first part, the almost incredibly brutal and completely
unsubstantiated attack on Lady Macclesfield, what extenuation
can be found? Johnson's great French contemporary Denis
Diderot, probably the most perceptive critic of the work, was,
like others, taken aback by it:

This Countess of Macclesfield is a strange woman, persecuting a love-child with a rage sustained for many years, never extinguished, and founded on nothing. If a writer decided to introduce, in a play or a novel, a character of this kind, it would be booed. Nevertheless it is compatible with reality. Is reality then sometimes to be booed? Why not? Does it never deserve it?[21]

But the Lady Macclesfield of the *Life* was not based on reality. She did *not*, as Johnson asserts, initiate the divorce proceedings in order to "obtain her liberty." They were initiated by Macclesfield, anxious to protect his title and estate from being inherited by a boy unrelated to him. She did *not* shamelessly proclaim her adultery; on the contrary, she defended herself vigorously. As Diderot points out, she had no discernible motive for persecuting her son. Indeed, Johnson admits as much:

It is natural to enquire upon what motives his mother would persecute him in a manner so outrageous and implacable; for what reason she would employ all the arts of malice and all the snares of calumny, to take away the life of her own son, of a son who never injured her. . . . Only this can be observed from her conduct, that the most execrable crimes are sometimes committed without apparent temptation.[22]

Which is a sad confession from a would-be psychobiographer. There is no evidence of her displaying any hostility against her daughter by Rivers (of whose existence Johnson was not even aware). "Warm maternal feelings were characteristic of her," Tracy sums her up. "She was a simple, domestic type of person, not the sort to be suspected of a grand passion. . . . For more than twenty-five years she endured the outcry Savage"—and Johnson—"raised against her. . . . She died insulted in her very obituary by a raking up of the scandal of her youth. Yet she never attempted to defend herself against his charges."[23]

All this libelous material Johnson took over uncritically from the anonymous 1727 *Life* and other propaganda put forward by Savage and his friends in hope of obtaining a pardon for him, although the facts about the Macclesfield divorce were on public record and could have been gathered by Johnson with a little serious research. Can it be excused by the very plausible suggestion that Johnson himself greatly resented his mother's domineering over him in his youth?[24] In spite of the handful of tender letters he wrote to her when she was on her deathbed at the age of ninety in 1759, for nearly twenty years he never managed to make the not very arduous journey from London to Lichfield to see her (after her death he made many of them). He once admitted to a friend that "he had never sought to please till past thirty years"—that is, until he had left Lichfield for London—"considering the matter as hopeless." Presumably it was old Sarah Johnson who had convinced him that it was hopeless. If so, we seem to have the psychobiographer hoist with his own psychobiography. But then recent years have seen a number of Freud's doctrines and psychiatric procedures explained as the consequences of his own upbringing.

The remainder of the *Account* consists chiefly of descriptions of Savage's behavior and the (usually unfortunate) results of it, and curious alternations of condemnation and condonation of it. As time goes on (and as Johnson becomes better acquainted with Savage), the condemnations tend to become more severe—indeed at times rather sarcastic. But even toward the end, Savage remains a man more sinned against than sinning. After his pardon for murder, he was

> as before, without any other support than accidental favours and uncertain patronage afforded him; sources by which he was sometimes very liberally supplied, and which at other times were suddenly stopped [usually because of some outrageous conduct against Savage's benefactor]; so that he spent his life between want and plenty, or what was yet worse, between beggary and extravagance; for as whatever he received was the gift of chance, which might as well favour him at one time as another, he was tempted to squander what he had, because he always hoped to be immediately supplied.

One might think the moral of this is to find some way of life in which one's income is not the gift of chance. But no: it turns out to be the fault of Savage's benefactors. Johnson continues,

> Another cause of his profusion was the absurd kindness of his friends, who at once rewarded and enjoyed his abilities, by

treating him at taverns, and habituated him to pleasures which he could not afford to enjoy, and which he was not able to deny himself, though he purchased the luxury of a single night by the anguish of cold and hunger for a week.[25]

Poor suffering victim of kindness! Quotations of this kind could be multiplied many times. Sometimes Johnson sounds like a parody of a modern social worker, and one almost expects some of his accounts of Savage's bizarre self-defeating actions to be followed by "Of course, this was really a cry for help." Help, as Johnson fully documents, Savage received in abundance, but it did him little good. Diderot put it pointedly: "This work would have been delightful, with a subtlety comparable to that of the *Memoirs of the Comte de Grammont*"—Anthony Hamilton's superbly deadpan account of his brother-in-law, a sharp operator in the courts of Louis XIV and Charles II—"if the English author had set out to satirize his hero; but unfortunately he is in earnest."[26] As catty, and shrewd, a piece of criticism of Johnson as has ever been made.

If the villainous Lady Macclesfield sounds like a fantasized version of Mrs. Michael Johnson of Lichfield, Richard Savage often sounds like young Sam. When his friends take up a collection to buy Savage a much needed suit of clothes and, understandably cautious about giving him the money, pay it to the tailor who is to come and take his measurements, Savage comes to the lodging of a friend (Johnson, no doubt) in "the most violent agonies of rage," complaining "with the utmost vehemence of indignation, 'That they had sent for a tailor to measure him.' "[27] One immediately recollects the story of how, when Johnson's shoes at Oxford had disintegrated to the point where he could no longer attend lectures, and some kind-hearted fellow undergraduates tiptoed to his room to leave a new pair before his door, they were startled by having them hurled back at them as they went downstairs.[28] When Johnson notes that Savage rose late in the day, and then prolonged his visits "to unseasonable hours, disconcerting all the families into which he was admitted," one recalls the complaints of Mrs. Thrale and others at Johnson's own unseasonable hours and the disruption he caused in family routine. This might sound like a rebuke of Savage. But Johnson acidly continues, "This was an error in a place of commerce [Bristol], which all the charms of his conversation"—such as the night-owl Johnson too could contribute—"could not compensate; for what trader would purchase such satisfaction by the loss of solid gain, which must be the consequence of midnight merriment, as those hours which were gained at night were generally lost in the morning."[29] Even at the age of thirty-five there is still a good deal of the Bohemian about Johnson as well as Savage.

"SLOW RISES WORTH BY POVERTY DEPRESSED," Johnson had put (in capitals) into the mouth of Thales–Savage, no doubt expressing his own *saeva indignatio* at this fact, which he had encountered for many years. It may also be, as I and others have suggested, that by writing these two tirades, *London* and the *Account*, he may have purged some of that indignation from his system—though there were many times in his later life when the bad boy, the rebel with or without a cause, could be detected beneath the surface of the great "conservative." ("Here's to the next insurrection of the Negroes in the West Indies," he proclaimed,[30] to Boswell's horror.) What may be thought to be a gradual increase in the acerbity with which he reprimands Savage's antics toward the end of the work might indicate some sort of catharsis. But Johnson's great final paragraph makes no concession:

> Those are no proper judges of his conduct who have slumbered away their time on the down of plenty, nor will a wise man easily presume to say, "Had I been in Savage's condition, I should have lived, or written, better than Savage."

This apparently *is* how Johnson wished to conclude the work. In the printed text it is followed by a paragraph affirming that "those who, in confidence of superior capacities or attainments disregard the common maxims of life" should be "reminded that nothing will supply the want of prudence, and that negligence and irregularity, long continued, will make knowledge useless, wit ridiculous, and genius contemptible." Unimpeachable advice, of course. But one wonders why Johnson took the trouble, in a copy of the work preserved in the University of Glasgow Library, to prefix to this paragraph a marginal manuscript note, "Added."[31] By whom, or on whose advice? Cave, perhaps, concerned for sales and anxious not to antagonize the right-thinking?

It is magnificent; but is it biography?[32] The teaching of *Rambler* No. 60 that the biographer should enable his reader to empathize or identify with his subject is no doubt excellent in itself. But is there not a limit beyond which the historical facts may not be distorted to achieve this end? Perhaps no one now cares very much whether the image of so insignificant a figure of literary history as Savage—who would not be remembered at all today but for Johnson—has been glamorized. Or perhaps even if the memory of the historically unimportant Mrs. Brett has been assiduously blackened. (Though it might be interesting if some champion of women's rights were to compose an account, perhaps a historical novel, of the whole affair from her point of view. What else should a middle-aged matron be expected to do when a strange young man suddenly intrudes in her drawing room or boudoir except scream and call her servants or even the police?) It might be different if the subject were a writer of real importance, Joyce, say, or Eliot, or Hemingway—or Samuel Johnson. The question of how much fictionalizing should be tolerated from Boswell in his life of Johnson in order to make it "a good read" is still being debated.[33] Professor Temmer, I think, puts it well: "One is tempted to claim that Johnson does for Savage what Boswell will do for Johnson . . . namely, renew traditional formulations of archetypes, Johnson of the parasite, Boswell of the conversationalist . . . in short, 'existentialize' literary types into specific mortal men."[34] It might be well to repeat Strachey: "Human beings are too important to be treated as mere existentializations of literary types. They have a value which is eternal, and must be felt for its own sake."

CHAPTER TWO

James Boswell's
Life of Johnson

MAXIMILLIAN E. NOVAK

My first literary encounter with James Boswell came not in perusing the *Life of Johnson* or the *London Journal* but in glancing at the works of a nineteenth-century humorist named John Kendrick Bangs when I was an adolescent. In his latter day versions of dialogues of the dead, *The House-Boat on the Styx* and *The Pursuit of the House-Boat*, Samuel Johnson appears as a forceful figure among a select gathering of great men and women. In the company of Shakespeare and Queen Elizabeth, Julius Caesar and Francis Bacon, he still remains the dominating intellectual force he was among the members of the Club. Boswell, on the other hand, appears as the weakest of the shades. He sits silently, recording everything Johnson says. At one point he is accidentally knocked into the Styx, emerging even less solid in his wet state than he was before. Johnson treats him as if he were a servant. Ordered out of the room by Johnson at one point in the narrative, Boswell frets about missing something clever. When he is not copying down Johnson's conversation word for word, he publishes a newspaper for the inhabitants of Hades that no one reads. In short, he is a perfect portrait of a weak, ineffectual parasite, and Bangs makes his subservience to Johnson one of the more amusing aspects of the *Houseboat* series. Too bad that Bangs had it all wrong, for if Boswell had been the stumbling and stuttering literary servant to Samuel Johnson, fewer Johnsonians would be so angry with him.

Although Macaulay hailed the *Life of Johnson* as the greatest of all biographies, some critics insisted that Walter Jackson Bate's psychologically probing account of Johnson's career, which

31

appeared in 1977, was far superior to Boswell's work. And while Donald Greene, the most forceful Johnson scholar of the twentieth century, had his reservations about Bate's effort, he has been attacking Boswell's *Life* for several decades. Whatever virtues Boswell's *Life* possessed, Greene argued, it could not be considered an adequate *biography* of Johnson. Professor Greene was kind enough to call my attention to a recent article by Germaine Greer in which the case against Boswell is presented in the kind of vivid language that most academics tend to avoid. Greer's style aside, she manages to express the virulence that some scholars have felt about Boswell's literary execution of what they regard as the *real* Samuel Johnson.

Greer starts her essay with an attack on literary biography in general. The main difficulty with the genre is that it distracts our attention from what is truly important about any writer— his literary productions. If a biography makes us spend our time on some scandal or silly event having nothing to do with literature, it must be regarded as serving a negative purpose. "Other kinds of biography," she writes, "may have some useful function: literary biography has none. Of all the biographical organisms, literary biography is the most predatory, the laziest and the least enterprising, for its subject is the most accessible and the most vulnerable."[1] The disease ("microbe") began with Boswell, she argues, and spread like the black death. Why is Boswell's *Life* respected as a great biography? The only reason she can imagine is that "Johnson is deemed to live in his pages," but she regards that as a betrayal of the true Johnson— Johnson the author who once lived on earth and was the most respected writer of his time. If he is to be found today, she maintains, it must be in his own pages, not in those of a writer known to contemporary audiences mainly for the scandalous, intimate details of his *Tour of the Hebrides*.

This element of scandal and gossip irritates Greer because she finds it the dreariest substitute for the living thought of Johnson:

A gossip columnist of my acquaintance told me that he liked Boswell, because Boswell was just like him. Precisely. In recasting Johnson's self and voice in his own style, Boswell revenged himself for being less remarkable, less perspicacious, less magnanimous than his subject, and then sniffed and salivated over the outcome. What posterity has accepted is Johnson passed through the bowels of Boswell. What lives, in this version, is not Johnson but Boswell's intestinal flora.

I make no apologies for the use of cloacal imagery, for none is more pertinent to the process which we are discussing. If you were to consider these grisly transmutations as taking place in the mind of the biographer, you might persuade yourself to think of them as harmless, tolerable. But the law of diminishing returns cannot be bucked; transmitted through Boswell, Johnson became less. *The Vanity of Human Wishes* and *London* are worth all of Boswell's scribbling but they remain unread. Boswell is easier to take.[2]

Greer sees Boswell as turning our attention from one of the truly great English writers toward a concern with what was most trivial in his life and personality. The tendency, she argues, is to reduce all that constitutes profound thought to some aspect of character. And having reduced ideas to elements of personality, the reader of literary biography may feel relieved of any compulsion to read the writings of the author whose life has been captured in fascinating detail by the biographer. Boswell is read while Johnson's writings gather dust; lives of Byron appear in great number and find an audience while "*Don Juan*, the greatest comic poem in English, remains unread."

I have quoted Germaine Greer at length because she expresses in vivid language what many Johnsonians feel but are reluctant to state for fear of injuring the feelings of their colleagues who love Boswell. But there is surely a certain amount of personal pique in what she writes. What feminist has not been told at some time or other that her ideas proceed not from a disinterested evaluation of the situation of women in the modern world but from some personal problem that has prevented her fulfilling her true role as a woman? The road from irritation over such self-satisfied effrontery to anger at the entire personal process of literary biography seems obvious enough. This does not mean that her arguments are wrong, but it suggests that we should examine them carefully.[3] After all, not many Johnsonians are ready to give up on literary biography entirely, for who practiced that genre with greater power than Johnson himself?

The first point that should be stressed is that Greer's vision seems to owe a good deal to the review-essay that Thomas

Babington Macaulay wrote on John Croker Wilson's edition of Boswell's *Life* in 1831. With the confidence of an age that seemed to think it had reinvented existence itself and rejected everything the previous century had to offer as naive or unnatural, Macaulay viewed Johnson as a writer whose reputation had been great but whose ideas could be dispensed with by a wiser era. He had a "strong but enslaved understanding." His style was excessively formal, awkward, "offensive" and not his natural way of speaking. While Macaulay allowed Johnson some degree of greatness, he instanced his attitude toward the French and French civilization as an example of his provinciality. He is to be remembered not for his writings but for his oddities and eccentricities—for his peculiar character. No wonder that he considered that Boswell had preserved everything of Johnson that need be known!

And of course, he dumped every possible insult on the head of poor Boswell, creating the paradox that his greatness as a biographer depended on his being "a great fool." Boswell was the "laughingstock" of that brilliant society around Johnson which lives today only because Boswell recorded its conversations. "He was always laying himself at the feet of some eminent man, and begging to be spit upon or trampled upon." He paraded about the Shakespeare Jubilee of 1769 with a sign identifying himself as "Corsican Boswell." He had no redeeming qualities: "Logic, eloquence, wit, taste, all these things which are generally considered as making a book valuable, were utterly wanting to him." And in one section Macaulay falls into a near poetic rhapsody of abuse in a display of that amplitude that constitutes the best and worst of Victorian prose:

> Servile and impertinent, shallow and pedantic, a bigot and a sot, bloated with family pride, and eternally blustering about the dignity of a born gentleman, yet stooping to be a tale-bearer, an eavesdropper, a common butt in the taverns of London, so curious to know everybody who was talked about, that, Tory and high Churchman as he was, he manoeuvred, we have been told, for an introduction to Tom Paine, so vain of the most childish distinctions, that when he had been to court, he drove to the office where his book was printing without changing his clothes, and summoned all the

printer's devils to admire his new ruffles and sword: such was this man, and such he was content and proud to be.[4]

What really bothered Macaulay about Boswell was the openness of his nature. Macaulay makes his candidness and frankness into marks of mental impotence: "He was perfectly frank, because the weakness of his understanding and the tumult of his spirits prevented him from knowing when he made himself ridiculous." His fame, which owed much to the degree of self revelation in the *Life* and elsewhere was close to "infamy." The paradox that his being "a dunce, a parasite, and a coxcomb" made him immortal as a biographer, does not prevent Macaulay from blasting him with one verbal broadside after another. Boswell was certainly everything that the Victorians detested. He lacked a sense of decorum, and ideals of duty and dedicated labor were but a small part of his personality. Macaulay's "slave" made for good comedy in Bangs' series, but that it should still pervade the work of a twentieth-century critic is surprising. If Germaine Greer believes that Boswell was hardly more than a gossip columnist and that he is somehow responsible for Macaulay's judgment that a quaint Samuel Johnson is best preserved in his *Life*, she should reconsider the sources of her attitudes. Eighteenth-century scholars have spent most of this century trying to free themselves from the efforts of Victorian critics to reduce their period to a few generalizations and then pretend its only importance lay in preparing the way for the greatness of their era. We must suspect any admirer of Johnson who takes the same position on Boswell as Macaulay.

Another difficulty with Greer's argument lies in the Gresham's law theory of literature—bad books drive out good. Does anyone believe that the person who takes pleasure in the more kinky aspects of Byron's sexual life is the likeliest reader of *Don Juan*? Why Greer selected Byron as an example for her argument is easy enough to see. Byron is almost unique in the history of literature in having established a direct link between his personality and his writings—between Byronism and the figures of Childe Harold and Don Juan. In some ways, the Byronic posture is almost a replacement for his literature. He was the first poet to put forward the image of the romantic artist as hero, and being handsome, witty, and completely shocking to bourgeois sensibilities, he may be said to have expressed more of his essential self in his life than in his art. But what has this to do with Samuel Johnson?

The Johnson that Boswell had in mind was not merely his friend of twenty years but the author of *The Idler* and *The Rambler*, of the great prefaces to Shakespeare and to the *Dictionary*, of *Rasselas* and *The Vanity of Human Wishes*. No one who has carefully read these works and his political pamphlets will think that Boswell, or perhaps a handful of thinkers in the history of the human race, could approach Johnson in the incisiveness of his view of literature or the profundity of his understanding of the human condition. If he showed a disproportionate amount of the human side of Johnson, it was because he thought that such a view would complement what he believed to be the obvious genius of his friend and subject. If Macaulay believed that Johnson's thought might be dispensed with and Boswell's study of the man put in its place, that was *his* problem, not Boswell's. The Johnson that Boswell presented was anything but the romanticized image of the writer projected by Byron. Boswell's Johnson was intended to supplement our understanding of the writings, not to replace them.

In what sense may it be argued, then, that the insubstantial biographical fare of Boswell has drawn readers away from the admittedly fuller menu provided by Johnson? It might be thought that but for Boswell more time in schools and colleges might be devoted to reading Johnson. This may seem the more plausible since terms are only so long and only so much can be read by students during a limited period of time. But most students sample Johnson and Boswell in classes offering an historical survey of literature. The competition in such classes, I would suspect, is more likely to involve a choice between how much time ought to be devoted to Swift or Pope or to Coleridge and Keats than whether Johnson may be given to students exclusively after he has passed through the intestines of Boswell, if one may utilize Germaine Greer's image. The *Life* may sometimes be used to extend a reading of Johnson, but what important anthology of major authors has substituted Boswell for Johnson? If Johnson is not read as widely as he ought to be, the fault will probably be found in modern reading tastes. And while readers of lives of Byron may feel little desire to examine Byron's poetry, the reader of Boswell's *Life* who does not want to read further in Johnson's writings must be remarkably lacking in curiosity.

Whereas Greer associates Boswell's *Life* with literary biography in general, there are those who, in attacking Boswell, would distinguish between certain types of literary biography. In this scheme, literary biography is a useful form of knowledge but Boswell's work would have to be given a different classification. Too limited in its scope and too intertwined with Boswell's own experiences, the *Life* might be classified as a personal memoir or as Boswell's private meditation on Johnson's life. In this scheme of things, the literary biographer is simply a version of the objective historian, hoping for an occasional insight that might raise the account of his or her subject above that of other accounts but a writer tied exclusively to the facts.

Such a concept may occasionally pass for wisdom among literary historians, but most historians long ago abandoned the idea that an historical narrative could ever be reduced to something so seemingly artless. George F. Kennan, the American diplomat and writer on foreign affairs, recently commented on the ideal of biography that would put it outside the reach of the literary. In such a scheme, the biographer is "no more than an intermediary between ascertainable fact and the reader. Let him be honored for his industry, for his patience, for the fortitude he has shown in burrowing around these dusty reliquiae and making some of them available to us with his critical commentary. And if, in doing this, he happens to have written here and there a few amusing sentences, let us give a gracious nod of recognition in his direction. . . . But let us not confuse things by putting his achievements on a plane with the great works of independent creative genius to which we give the name of literature." Having described so well the ideal compared to which, in the mind of Donald Greene and others, Boswell's work fails so miserably, Kennan confesses that in practice the matter is not "so simple."[5] To make his work interesting and, in some sense, more true, the biographer is always picturing what is merely probable rather than certain. And he is inevitably trapped in the views of his time and position.

The difficulty is that even if the biographer assumes the most humble role in relation to his subject, such a stance is just that—one role among many that might be selected. In his study of the novel, *The Rhetoric of Fiction*, Wayne Booth demonstrated that the idea of an invisible narrator in the novel—an ideal which appeared in both the most sophisticated criticism and in the popular handbooks for writing fiction, was merely sleight of hand, a rhetorical device. Fiction, he argued, is a form of statement, and the narrator is always present, telling us what and how to think of the characters and the world in which they move. Flaubert's juxtaposition of the market scene, with its mixture of vulgarity, bestiality and absurdity, alongside his account of Madame Bovary's first great affair, makes as thorough a statement as the typical sermon with which George Eliot closes a chapter of *Middlemarch*. Booth maintained that novelists who fail to clarify their position about character and event are guilty of failing in their responsibility to the reader.[6] It is an abrogation of the contract between the author and the reader. Not everyone agreed with Booth on the moral responsibility of the writer, but his work resulted in a shift to an examination of authorial meaning and intent. Recent interest in fiction has focused on Bakhtin's dialogic view of fiction in which characters have their separate voices and may even represent different literary modes in a kind of debate.

The importance of this critical discussion for biography should be obvious. There is no such thing as an invisible biographer. Instead of striving after an illusory objectivity, then, should he not admit his presence in the work and offer his judgments as honestly as possible? Would Boswell's *Life* have been better had he aimed at being an "invisible" narrator? The answer has to be a resounding no. Boswell inherited from his time a distrust of history. He thought that the best approach he could take would be to be as true to himself as he could be in presenting Johnson's career and character. Instead of a rhetorical objectivity, he gave the reader his ideas, opinions, criticisms of Johnson. Germaine Greer is right to argue that Mrs. Thrale knew Johnson better than Boswell, but who ever thought her collection of Johnson's opinions a masterpiece? Boswell succeeded so brilliantly because he obeyed the injunctions of an Age of Sensibility to begin any task by being sincere—being true to one's real self in a somewhat different way from the ancient injunction—"know thyself."

Boswell's enthusiasm for great men was so general, that we may pass over his attempt to convince Rousseau of his discipleship as just another episode in his collection of great

masters: Hume, Johnson, Voltaire, Paoli, etc. But Robert
Darnton has shown how completely some people dedicated
themselves to living a more open life of feeling under the
influence of Rousseau.[7] He tells of one disciple who remained
silent for three months to avoid what Rousseau believed to be a
certain blockage in the path to natural emotion introduced by
language.[8] Other followers dedicated themselves to giving their
children the kind of education that Rousseau advocated in
Emile. Before 1764, when Boswell came to see Rousseau, he had
apparently read little that Rousseau had written and had to
engage in a rapid perusal of *Emile* and *La Nouvelle Héloïse*. But
Rousseau's reputation was at its height, and the principles with
which he was associated were well known. As Frederick Pottle
stated, "Boswell came to Rousseau as a disciple to a master, as
a patient to a physician, in a sense as a penitent to a confessor."[9]
Both shared that appreciation for sincere emotion that was the
key to the Age of Sensibility.

Boswell recorded his expectations of the interview in typical
fashion:

> my romantic genius, which will never be extinguished, made
> me eager to put my own merit to the severest trial. I had
> therefore prepared a letter to Monsieur Rousseau, in which I
> informed him that an ancient Scots gentleman of twenty-four
> was come hither with the hopes of seeing him. I assured him
> that I deserved his regard, that I was ready to stand the test
> of his penetration. Towards the end of my letter I showed
> him that I had a heart and a soul. I have here given no idea
> of my letter. It can neither be abridged nor transposed, for it
> is really a masterpiece. I shall ever preserve it as a proof that
> my soul can be sublime. I dressed and dined and sent my
> letter *chez* Monsieur Rousseau, ordering the maid to leave it
> and say she'd return for the answer, so that I might give him
> time to consider a little, lest perhaps he might be ill and
> suddenly refuse to see me. I was filled with anxiety. Is not
> this romantic madness: Was I not sure of admittance by my
> recommendations? Could I not see him as any other gentleman
> would do? No: I am above the vulgar crowd. I would have
> my merit fairly tried by this great judge of human nature. I
> must have things in my own way. If my bold attempt
> succeeds, the recollection of it will be grand as long as I live.

But perhaps I may appear to him so vain, or so extraordinary, that he may be shocked by such a character and may not admit me. I shall then be in a pretty situation, for I shall be ashamed to present my recommendations. But why all this doubt and uneasiness? It is the effect of my melancholy timidity. What! can the author of *Eloisa* be offended at the enthusiasm of an ingenuous mind? But if he does admit me, I shall have a very difficult character to support; for I have written to him with unusual elevation, and given him an idea of me which I shall hardly come up to.[10]

Would anyone but Boswell have recorded the fluctuation of his feelings as he awaited Rousseau's reaction to his letter? Boswell reveals himself as a complete fool, but he also shows himself as completely human. What person does not have these fluctuations of emotions? How many were capable of revealing them so well? Boswell eventually got Rousseau to listen to the story of his affair with a married woman in Scotland. He spoke of looking for a priest to whom he could confess his feelings. Instead he confessed them to Rousseau.

Boswell was an ideal example of a particular kind of sensibility. He tended to present himself as an "enthusiast," as a man of feeling, but he was far from the character, Harley, Mackenzie's hero of the popular novel of that name. Harley trembles with sensibility at the sight of every human sadness. Boswell, an egotist when he was not suffering from depression or hypochondria, had his sensibility focused entirely on himself and his emotions.[11] His description of his feelings on awaiting Rosseau's response to his letter mingled anxiety with expectation, vanity with a fear of failure, a compulsion to place himself in embarrassing situations with an excitement over the prospect of success. In the context of the age, Harley's sensibility was idealized as all that might have been expected of a virtuous young man possessed of a profound sensibility, but the age also had characters such as the unhappy nephew of Rameau in Diderot's novel—men of deep sensibility whose mediocre talents and bitterness prefigured the ideal recipient for the message of fascism in the twentieth century.

Rousseau himself was a man possessed of an ambivalent sensibility. His ability to make himself ridiculous along with his capacity to alienate those who approached him with the best intentions suggests the many-sidedness of sensibility in the period. Whatever he did, from putting his five children into an orphanage to making Voltaire into an implacable enemy, no one doubted the true sensibility of Boswell's "wild" philosopher. Given Boswell's character, he might have been more suited to writing a biography of Rousseau than of Samuel Johnson, but his choice of subject arose from an admiration for the control that he lacked, for the principles which he could hold only with "some degree of relaxation,"[12] and for the solidity of character which he could never find within himself. To wish that Boswell might have selected a different subject in order to spare us a Johnson written from what is admittedly a somewhat odd perspective is to wish away the complexities of the age itself.

What we have in Boswell as the narrator of the *Life of Johnson*, then, is a man practicing a particular form of sensibility, the most obvious aspect of which was his combination of egotism and depression, or, as he would have put it, vanity and hypochondria. In his *Letter to the People of Scotland* (1785), he paused to confess one side of his personality. "Allow me to indulge a little my *own egotism* and *vanity*," he wrote. "They are the indigenous plants of my mind: they distinguish it. I may prune their luxuriancy; but I must not entirely clear it of them; for then I should be no longer as I am; and there might be something not so good."[13] Such confessions are commonplace in both his published writings and his journals. If they sometimes seem ludicrous, it is partly because we have become accustomed to psychoanalytic terminology in any self-analysis and partly because Boswell often seems to regard the private Boswell, the Boswell whom he addresses in his journals, as another self to whom he can speak with intimacy. Occasionally, as in his self-characterization within the *Tour*, he seems to be courting a kind of embarrassment:

> He was then in his thirty-third year, and had been about four years happily married. His inclination was to be a soldier, but his father, a respectable Judge, had pressed him into the profession of the Law. He had travelled a good deal and seen many varieties of human life. He had thought more than any body supposed, and had a pretty good stock of general learning and knowledge. He had all Dr. Johnson's principles, with some degree of relaxation. He had rather too little than

too much prudence, and his imagination being lively, he
often said things of which the effect was very different from
the intention.[14]

What degree of relaxation? Was it commonly rumored that he
had not thought at all? Is this passage, which borders on the
ludicrous, a deliberate attempt to reveal the kind of thing that
would be misconstrued and laughed at? Sometimes he would
give pages of his journal over to cheering himself up, and one of
the most encouraging things he would tell himself was that if he
was not a great man himself, his admiration for great men
could compensate for what he found lacking in his inner self.[15]
And when he had his biographical object in view, he experienced
a tremendous sense of exhilaration.

In his *Tour to the Hebrides*, he expressed and revealed feelings
in what he called a "ludicrous" image. "I was elated by the
thought of having been able to entice such a man to this remote
part of the world," he stated. "A ludicrous, yet just image
presented itself to my mind, which I expressed to the company.
I compared myself to a dog who has got hold of a large piece of
meat, and runs away with it to a corner, where he may devour
it in peace, without fear of others taking it from him."[16] Though
his rejoicing in having Johnson to himself is part of his emotion,
he also shows no inconsiderable delight in the control he has
over Johnson in this situation. He uses less graphic imagery in
the same work in expressing his handling of Johnson's prejudices
against Scotland. Depicting himself as a very different kind of
person, as "a citizen of the world" above petty nationalistic
prejudices, he remarks that when he encounters such prejudice
against his native land, he humors the speaker: "I fairly own I
treat them as children. And thus I have, at some moments,
found myself to treat even Dr. Johnson."[17] The Boswell who
wrote that sentiment is a far cry from the pale shade of Bangs'
Houseboat.

One seeming oddity is that Johnson apparently had no
objection to Boswell's efforts, even if he did not actually
encourage them. In one letter he urged Boswell not to burn
some of his more intimate material, and he looked over much of
what appeared in Boswell's *Tour to the Hebrides*, though it was
published after his death. At one point in the biography,
Boswell asked Johnson's judgment upon his method of collecting

biographical material and received an encouraging reply: "I asked Johnson whether a man's being forward in making himself known to eminent people, and seeing as much of life, and getting as much information as he could in every way, was not yet lessening himself by his forwardness. JOHNSON. 'No, Sir; a man always makes himself greater as he increases his knowledge.' "[18] That Johnson burned many of his own papers before his death is beside the point. He probably saw in Boswell the living exemplar of the kind of biographer he would have wanted—a biographer devoted to telling the truth and to finding the truth in small details of behavior. When Boswell wanted to explain his biographical method, he quoted at length from Johnson's essay on that subject, *Rambler* No. 60. In that essay, Johnson alluded to the sentiments of Chief Justice Hale, who noted that whenever he felt pity for a criminal, he recalled the pity due to the nation at large who were the victims of the criminal. "If we owe regard to the memory of the dead," Johnson continued, "there is yet more respect to be paid to knowledge, to virtue and to truth."[19] In selecting the image of pity felt for a criminal, Johnson was probably thinking in terms of an execution, and he may well have felt that the ideal biography ought to spare no one. He must have had some idea of the kind of biography that Boswell would write, and his unwillingness to act as a censor of Boswell's projects may suggest that he was willing to sacrifice himself in the name of truth.

Boswell's image of carrying off Johnson like a dog making off with a piece of meat along with his way of treating Johnson at times as a child embodies some fundamental contradictions which deserve further comment. Boswell casts himself in the biography as an ardent disciple of Johnson and as something of a foster son. It is as the heir to Johnson's wisdom and principles that he fights off the claims of Sir John Hawkins and Hester Lynch Piozzi, who also pretended to be the keepers of Johnson's biographical estate. The one, he suggests, hardly knew Johnson, while the other tended to present her anecdotes about Johnson without a proper context.[20] As Johnson's friend for twenty years and as the person whom Johnson knew to be writing his biography, only he had the right to speak for the master. And with the success of his biography he could boast, "I have *Johnsonised* the land; and I trust [his readers] will not only *talk* but *think* Johnson."[21] No critic of Boswell's *Life* has questioned his ardent devotion to Johnson; what is in question is his judgment of Johnson's character and mind.

Boswell took Johnson as his surrogate father. He found dealing with his real father, the "respectable judge," impossible. His entire sense of self seemed to disintegrate in the presence of that disapproving authority figure, Alexander Boswell, eighth Lord of Auchinleck. In the sense outlined by Heinz Kohut, he could not find in his father the proper mirror to guide his own ideal image of himself. He was almost compulsive in doing things that would result in his father's stern disapproval. Kohut tells of a patient who dreamed that he was wandering without guidance inside a great icy heart and found himself on exiting through a crack in an even more terrible, stainless steel world of principled isolation. The dreamer felt the anxiety of never finding anyone he could trust or who would return his affection.[22] To some extent, the dreamer might have been Boswell before his meeting with Johnson. In Johnson he found a man of literary fame, a fast and sympathetic friend, and a teacher. Johnson could lay claim to being a moral philosopher whose pronouncements would have more weight than those of his actual father, and his apparent acceptance of Boswell's foibles relieved some of the anxiety that he felt about himself.

At the same time, Boswell, as the heir of Auchinleck, could feel superior in birth, wealth and manners to the bear-like Johnson, whose appearance in well-worn clothes and an old wig often dismayed his visitors. Boswell was also young and vigorous while Johnson had weak eyesight and was beginning to lose his hearing by the time he travelled to Scotland in 1773 with Boswell. He had suffered from scrofula as a child and was given to all kinds of tics and involuntary motions. After a vivid description of Johnson's eating habits and appearance while devouring his food, "the veins of his forehead swelled, and generally a strong perspiration was visible," a description that has some of the quality of Gulliver's account of the Brobdingnagian giants at their meals, Boswell commented, "To those whose sensations were delicate, this could not but be disgusting; and it was doubtless not very suitable to the character of a philosopher, who should be distinguished by self-command."[23] From such remarks, Boswell's occasional sense of superiority to Johnson should be obvious. Unlike a real father,

Johnson could be tested, probed, maneuvered into awkward situations. Occasionally Boswell would exceed the limits of what Johnson would endure, as if there were times when he needed to feel a certain anxiety about their relationship. Then, like an affectionate parent who will forgive his child almost everything, Johnson would persuade Boswell of his continued affection for him. In turn, Boswell showed Johnson continual evidence of the warmth of his regard.

Boswell's sudden fancy about being a dog and carrying off Johnson as a piece of meat all for himself has profound significance. It suggests his jealousy of rivals for Johnson's favor, his power over him, and his tendency to regard Johnson as something to be devoured. If it were simply Johnson's ethical ideas that Boswell wanted to take into himself, no one would object, but it is Johnson himself whom his biographer wants to gobble up. But Johnson was too large a portion to swallow. Gulliver could just as soon try to eat a Brobdingnagian meal as Boswell attempt to absorb Johnson. That is why the concern of so many Johnsonians seems misplaced.

Had he succeeded, the *Life* would read like Nabokov's *Pale Fire*, in which the fictional writer of notes to a work by a famous American poet transforms his commentary into an autobiography. There are moments when Boswell approaches this. He takes the occasion of Johnson's discussion of Horace with Wilkes to add several pages of notes, the purpose of which appears to be merely to show his own learning. He treats us to a display of his own narrowness of mind when he engages Johnson in his desire to see that the estate of Auchinleck be passed on only to male heirs. (Typically enough, Johnson came out on the side of allowing women the right to inherit property.) He indulges in a near manic display of vanity over the success of his biography in the advertisement for the second edition. He thinks nothing of upbraiding Johnson for his narrow views when Johnson speaks against slavery or of offering his own opinions on literature when he feels Johnson's are wanting. But Nabokov's Gradus was mad. Boswell did not deny himself a place in his work, but he wanted the world to see, to hear and to understand Johnson as he did, or, as he put it again, "to *think* and *talk* Johnson." The trouble is that were we to choose a guide to Johnson's thought, Boswell would be an unlikely candidate for the job. He was not good at ideas. He does not seem to have fully understood Johnson's politics, and while he claimed to be a follower of Johnson's moral principles the seriousness with which Johnson approached human existence seems to have been beyond him.

But as he boasted in the early pages of the biography, he excelled in recording details and if he was not very good in analyzing what Johnson was saying, he could recapture Johnson's conversation. We do not have to have very much of Johnson through Boswell's interpretation because he gives us so much of Johnson's actual dialogue when engaged in winning debates with his friends. If he tends to keep Johnson's manner of speaking consistent, somewhat like a character in a novel, we know by comparison with other accounts of Johnson in action that Boswell preserved the basic content of his remarks. Thus in the first meeting between Boswell and Johnson on that memorable Monday, May 16, 1763, Boswell dramatizes their first encounter in the bookshop of Thomas Davies in a manner that might be found objectionable. At the same time, Boswell eventually manages to set down what Johnson has to say on a number of important issues.

For example, Boswell's sense that Davies announced Johnson's coming in a manner similar to Horatio's informing Hamlet of the approach of his father's ghost may simply be a clue to Boswell's imagination at the time. Davies had been an actor, but any echo of the scene from *Hamlet* was probably Boswell's projection. That Boswell should have cast himself as Hamlet and Johnson as the ghost of his father suggests the role he was preparing for Johnson. The ghost, after all, delivers the message that relieves Hamlet from his aimless brooding and sets him on a purposeful course. And although terrified at first by the prospect of conversing with the ghost, Hamlet perseveres and is even able to jest at the echo of the ghost as he swears his friends to secrecy. Boswell also perseveres, though almost struck dumb by Johnson's twisting his account of being from Scotland into a sharp witticism. He stays to record Johnson's comment on society and the superior man:

> In barbarous society, superiority of parts is of real consequence. Great strength or great wisdom is of much value to an individual. But in more polished times there are people to do every thing for money; and then there are a

number of other superiorities, such as those of birth and fortune, and rank, that dissipate men's attention, and leave no extraordinary share of respect for person and intellectual superiority. This is wisely ordered by Providence, to preserve some equality among mankind.[24]

Johnson's sense of contemporary society as dominated by money and the way such a society tends to reduce everything to mediocrity is stated elsewhere, but who would want to lose this particular view? And who would want to lose Johnson's comment on the way the concepts of liberty and patriotism, as abstract concepts, raise no genuine emotion among the people? Both Boswell and Mrs. Thrale wished that all of Johnson's conversation could be preserved for posterity. Who can regret that Boswell was there to capture so much of Johnson's thought?

I used to think that one of Boswell's talents was to ask slightly dumb questions by which he succeeded in getting Johnson's most outraged responses. When examined carefully, however, most of these queries tie in with the concerns of the late eighteenth century. For example, Johnson boasts that though he is sixty-eight, he has little of the mannerisms of old age in his conversation. Boswell then raises the kind of question that drew out the best in Johnson's thinking:

BOSWELL. But Sir, would not you wish to know old age? He who is never an old man, does not know the whole of human life; for old age is one of the divisions of it.
JOHNSON. Nay, Sir, what talk is this?
BOSWELL. I mean, Sir, the Sphinx's description of it;— morning, noon, and night. I would know night, as well as morning and noon.
JOHNSON. What, Sir, would you know what it is to feel the evils of old age? Would you have the gout? Would you have decrepitude?
Seeing him heated, I would not argue any farther; but I was confident that I was in the right. I would, in due time, be a Nestor, an elder of the people; and there *should* be some difference between the conversation of twenty-eight and sixty eight. A grave picture should not be gay. There is a serene, solemn, placid old age.[25]

Now within the context of eighteenth-century thought the

freedom to experience everything that was considered natural was
a precious right. Johnson himself allows his fictional protagonist,
Rasselas, to experience the varieties of existence before
concluding that happiness is not an attainable state. Boswell had
a right to feel that he was on better philosophical grounds than
Johnson. But this was the kind of moment when Johnson would
advise Boswell, "Clear your mind of cant."[26] To philosophize
about old age as part of the natural cycle of existence is easy
enough, but to suffer the realities of old age—sickness, pain,
forgetfulness—is quite another thing. No wonder Johnson
becomes "heated."

The scene also has a rich dramatic tension. It begins with
Johnson's praise of Ramsay, "in whose conversation there is more
instruction, more information, and more elegance" than of
anyone he knows. Boswell then introduces the idea of age
remarking, "What I admire in Ramsay, is his continuing to be so
young." Johnson's willingness to grant this as a virtue suggests
something of the longing of age after youth and the conversation of
youth, and his praise of his own conversation as having the quality
of a man of twenty-eight—neither repetitious nor unduly dwelling
on the superiority of the past to the present—should bring a
compliment from his young friend. Instead, it brings out Boswell's
speculation about the potential happiness of old age, a happiness
born of wisdom and experience. He is once more acting his
role—that of a young innocent man full of hope—and unlike
Johnson, is thinking more of the content than the mannerisms of
what *his* conversation would be like when he reached Johnson's
age. I doubt if he knew that he sounded a little like Gulliver in
expectation of meeting the Struldbruggs, those creatures cursed
from birth with the gift of living for hundreds of years without the
accompanying benefit of a youthfulness of mind and body.
Gulliver is horrified to discover that the Stuldbruggs suffer all the
pains and senility of old age and that their longevity merely
intensifies their suffering and isolation. Johnson's reaction to
Boswell's optimism strikes the reader with much the same force.
That Boswell did not revise his comment is odd, since the "placid
old age" that he considered possible in 1778 was clearly an
unlikely reality in the years to come.

To deny Boswell his due in scenes of this kind would be a grave
mistake. If the effect be put down to a simple recording of events,
we should remember that he raises the issues that produce the

response. His persistent introduction of the subject of death, despite his knowledge of Johnson's terror of dying, eventually produces so violent a reaction from Johnson that he tells Boswell not to visit him the next day. And the most outrageously staged scene involved the successful ploy by which he managed to bring Johnson to sit at the same table with the arch Whig, John Wilkes, the manufacturer of "liberty" as a popular cry among the people. Boswell's cheeky approach to this event recalls the dog-meat image. The scene is unnatural and contrived and only its reality makes it believable. It has the drama of opposition with which Boswell structures so much in his picture of Johnson's character—Johnson's almost freakish outward appearance played against his inner brilliance, his rough exterior contrasted with his heart of gold, the poverty of his clothes compared with the richness of his spirit. Though the scene with Wilkes has abundant drama, it suffers from forcing art upon life just a bit too much. The *Life of Johnson* is one of those works which is most successful where it captures the rush of events and ideas and somehow gives us an impression that, as readers, we are experiencing something close to life itself. Johnson's meeting with Wilkes has a bit of the contrived quality and inevitability of such Hollywood double sequels as *Frankenstein Meets the Wolfman*.

Aside from boasting about his ingenuity in reproducing Johnson's conversation, Boswell chiefly prided himself on his technique of piling up details about Johnson, arguing that such a "Flemish" technique was aesthetically valid and pleasing. "I remain firm and confident in my opinion," he wrote, "that minute particulars are frequently characteristick, and always amusing, when they relate to a distinguished man."[27] In this belief, Boswell shared a principle that was common to the aesthetics of the second half of the eighteenth century but which had its detractors then and now. Both Johnson and Reynolds held to a theory of art that advocated generalizing and idealization. The quarrel took definite shape during the Renaissance when the Italian artists expressed their contempt for northern European painting as being unimaginative. Anyone could paint what might be viewed in nature. "They paint stuffs and masonry, the green grass of the fields, the shadow of trees, and rivers and bridges, which they call landscapes, with many figures on this side and many figures on that," wrote Michelangelo. "And all this, though it pleases some persons, is done without reason or art, without symmetry or proportion, without skilful choice or boldness and, finally, without substance or vigour."[28] Similarly, Sir Joshua Reynolds, a friend of both Johnson and Boswell, argued that the Dutch painters, including Rembrandt, practiced an inferior kind of art. They captured nature as it was, but their attempt to create "exact representations of individual objects with all their imperfections" was misguided. They were operating under a wrong theory and were doomed to create paintings in "bad taste."[29] Samuel Johnson, who was a major influence on Reynolds, held the same attitude on literature associated with the classical genres, attacking excessive particularity and praising lines and sentiments that found a "mirror" in the minds of readers. But was biography a different matter even for Johnson, whose name Boswell evokes as his mentor in biography?

In treating fictive forms, Johnson argued that the primary requirement of the writer was moral—since the writer had the power to create stories as he wished, his duty to his society required that he demonstrate the triumph of good over evil. To show the opposite was authentic but unethical. Hence his disapproval of the ending to *King Lear* and of those modern novels which, in his eyes, did not inculcate a strong enough moral. In history and biography there was no way of changing the facts, but the author had the obligation to keep his judgment active at all times, indicating to his readers what he considered to be right behavior. Johnson's lives have only the roughest organization, usually comprising a chronological account and, at least in his *Lives of the Poets*, a critical assessment of the works and the career. But his powers of generalization and his judgment on various points of a poet's actions are ever present.

Despite his evocation of Johnson as his guide for biography, Boswell used a completely different method. His true model should have been the realistic novels of Defoe and Richardson, for in the piling up of detail and his surrender to the randomness of conversation and action, he brings biography to the support of realistic fiction. And he did this at a time when detailed description in the novel was becoming the province of Gothic romance in which it functioned, for the most part, as an anti-realistic device. He evoked Homer's *Odyssey* and the epic as a comparable form, but his willingness to incorporate whole letters and even Johnson's notes on his journey to France bears some resemblance to Richardson. For that novelist incorporated into

Sir Charles Grandison entire blocks of correspondence from the past as a means of moving backwards in time in a form oriented so strongly to the present. As for the kind of generalization and judgment about character that Johnson provides, Boswell simply cannot muster the authority which seemed to come so naturally from Johnson.

But just as he had a wonderful ear for Johnson's conversation, he also had a wonderful eye for what he considered to be a delightful detail. His early meetings with Johnson are instructive. When he sees Johnson at Davies' shop, he gives us an allusion rather than a description. "I found that I had a very perfect idea of Johnson's figure, from the portrait of him painted by Sir Joshua Reynolds soon after he had published his *Dictionary*, in the attitude of sitting in his easy chair in deep meditation, which was the first picture his friend did for him, which Sir Joshua very kindly presented to me, and from which an engraving has been made for this work."[30] Johnson's voice rather than his appearance is what we first learn about, and there is surely no accident in this. Only in the next meeting do we get a picture of the "uncouth" Johnson whose oddities become irrelevant as soon as he starts to speak:

> His brown suit of cloaths looked very rusty; he had on a little old shrivelled unpowdered wig, which was too small for his head; his shirt-neck and knees of his breeches were loose; his black worsted stockings ill drawn up; and he had a pair of unbuckled shoes by way of slippers. But all these slovenly particularities were forgotten the moment that he began to talk.[31]

And talk he does in Boswell's version of his life. Boswell is not content to give us what he says on a given occasion but, as with the conversation that followed his vivid "Flemish" description, he follows up on the topic of the poet, Christopher Smart, with another conversation on the same subject held at another time. Boswell's details sometimes involve physical description but more often than not they develop Johnson's opinions on literature and life. The wonderful collection of Johnson's opinions about eating come one after the other as he praises his own discernment, attacks someone who offended him by not inviting him to a sufficiently good meal and lavishes compliments on the cook of one of his friends. The context of all of this is Boswell's feeling that Johnson spent too much energy in thinking about food, but this objection is ploughed under by Johnson's exuberant pleasure in eating. The details make Johnson even more human than even he might have wanted to be.

Boswell was unique in his openness, but even he had secrets that he wanted to protect. The good biographer has to search for hidden motivation and hidden facts. As the subject of biography, Johnson's feelings and motives are dragged into the light to be subjected to something like an execution followed by an autopsy. Interestingly enough nothing fascinated Boswell so much as death, particularly an execution. On such occasions he seemed motivated by the kind of morbid curiosity dramatized in the Gothic romances of Mrs. Radcliffe. Radcliffe's heroines feel compelled to explore and probe what they know to be forbidden and dangerous. Moved by impulses they cannot explain, they ascribe their actions to "curiosity." As modern readers, we recognize the deeper psychological impulses behind their actions. Should anyone attempt to equate such ambiguous emotions with the kind of levity that moves readers of gossip columns, we would have no difficulty in seeing a failure to make discriminations.

Even more absurd is Greer's equation of Boswell's *Life of Johnson* with an extended gossip column. Johnson defended biography, both the writing and the reading of it, as an important kind of learning. To reduce the kind of curiosity that motivated Boswell to the titillation in uncovering gossip would be to misunderstand the layered meaning of that word for Boswell's age.[32] In revealing every detail about Johnson's life that he could discover through fact and speculation, Boswell was unquestionably indulging in what many contemporaries viewed as a public execution of his dead friend's character. But Boswell's *Life of Johnson* showed, as nothing of its kind before it, that biography can teach us what it means to be human. Unlike Plutarch's heroes, Johnson conquered no cities, fell in love with no person for whom an entire world would be worth sacrificing and died no glorious death. For Boswell Johnson was a true "hero" mainly because he was a great moralist and a great writer. What modern critic does not think that he knows more about the nature of Johnson's greatness than Boswell? But Boswell knew Johnson and loved him as a friend, and if the Johnson that he serves up to the reader is not to everyone's taste, we should never deny him that ability to convey the authentic joy and wisdom he experienced in Johnson's company.

CHAPTER THREE

Lytton Strachey's
Eminent Victorians

MILLICENT BELL

The "new biography" has long ceased to seem new, and when we reread *Eminent Victorians* now we are able to see that its extraordinary impact was hardly due to a violent break with the entire tradition of English biography. What sent shock waves through its first readers was the bold assumption, simply, of an attitude, a stance, which did not predicate veneration or even respect for its human subjects who were nothing less than parental figures to the readers themselves. An Oedipal aggression, cheerfully unashamed, voiced itself on behalf of a whole generation against those overbearing elders who had once compelled awe—and the sensation was delicious for Strachey's contemporaries as it cannot be for us, who have learned to look at the Victorians more sympathetically. Perhaps the interest of *Eminent Victorians* is thus chiefly historic; its most brilliant discovery may have been its ironic title and the perfection of its timing in 1918, when the Great War, as it was called, seemed to have concluded the bankruptcy of Victorian energy and moralism.

Strachey's quarrel with the immediately preceding generations of England was personal; was he not the child of a Victorian family with Evangelical traditions and with an eminent paterfamilias as its head? General Sir Richard Strachey, a man of prodigious industry, had developed railways, canals, a forest service and numerous other administrative improvements, in India. He was a soldier but also a botanist, meteorologist and mathematician. Lytton, the eleventh of his thirteen children, remembered him, even in his retirement, tirelessly at work at home making unending calculations at his encumbered desk.

53

Strachey's mother seems to have been, for her part, one of those women who administered her huge household with an effective domestic tyranny that reminded one that society's supreme symbol (if not actual source) of power was a woman. Not for nothing would Strachey's biography of the Queen exhibit an amused filial indulgence mingled with mockery. The cluttered family house at Lancaster Gate seemed to the young Strachey "one vast filth-packet, and we the mere *disjecta membra* of vanished generations, which Providence was too busy or too idle to clear away."[1] He felt it to be already fissured like the House of Usher, yet he grew up with the sense that it had stood firm until his own time.

Strachey must have known what is so obvious now, that the Victorian period was not monolithic. A vein of unease underlay the confident material progress and moral smugness of the era. Yet he seems to have felt that such doubts went unexpressed. "The Victorian Age, so great in so many directions, was not great in criticism, in humour, in the realistic apprehension of life. It was an age of complacency and self-contradiction,"[2] he wrote in an essay on Lord Morley. Yet the most eminent spokesmen of Victorian culture—Carlyle, Dickens, Arnold, Ruskin, Morris—were also its critics—though Strachey had a limited appreciation of this fact. He once recommended that "a club should be started—an Old Victorian Club—the business of whose members would be protect the reputation of their Age and give it a fair chance with the public. Perhaps such a club exists already—in some quiet corner of Pimlico; but if so, it has sadly neglected one of its most pressing duties—the hushing up of Matthew Arnold."[3]

At the last, in Wilde, something like Strachey's total scepticism had created a tone and a style of expression that anticipated his own. Wilde, the fellow-deviant, anticipated Strachey's personal distaste for moralistic humbug, shared his spoiled-dandy wit. But Strachey was not interested in finding admirations so near; if he identified any progenitors at all in the English tradition it was likely to be in the previous century, the eighteenth, when, whether in England or in France, he might have lived happily. Yet Wilde is a closer kin than Johnson. If Strachey shares with Johnson suspicion of that most pernicious of mankind's convictions, the conviction of its own virtue, Johnson, as Hugh Kingsmill observed, always seems to believe that absolute goodness exists somewhere, a sense lost to Wilde and Strachey.

Strachey had originally planned a "balanced" set of portraits which would include scientists or others to whom he might give some approval—as many as a dozen figures. But he settled with precision on four whom he could freely demolish: a distinguished Churchman who had embraced the Old Faith after contact with the Oxford Movement and risen to the highest eminence in the hierarchy of England; the greatest of Victorian do-gooders, a female saint; the greatest of Victorian schoolmasters, who had made the public school an instrument for the molding of "Christian Gentlemen" and rulers of empire; and the soldier–martyr who had died with epic courage at his private Thermopylae, Khartoum, and for whom the nation and its Queen had wept. That one could come to laugh at such personages was the greatest of revelations.

The Preface to *Eminent Victorians* boasts justly of its author's freedom from the compulsion to be complimentary. The obligation to speak no ill of the dead had weighed heavily even on the greatest biographers of the past century. Any critical frankness, like James Anthony Froude's in his biography of Carlyle, outraged contemporary prejudice. Elizabeth Gaskell's brilliant *Charlotte Brontë*, bold about some matters, was evasive about others. Strachey's announcement that he would "lay bare the facts . . . dispassionately, impartially, and without ulterior intentions"[4] was fortified by the fact that unlike most nineteenth-century biographers, from the hack writer to the literary professional, he had no allegiance to his subject, no obligations to widow or widower. When he came to do his portraits in *Eminent Victorians*, he could be satisfied that he was not, like Edmund Purcell, the fellow-religionist whom Manning himself had selected as his biographer, not, like Arthur Penrhyn Stanley, one of Thomas Arnold's favorite students, not, like Sir Edward Cook, the recipient of a vast mass of Nightingale's papers at the hands of a trusting family. Far from endorsing Carlyle's view in *Sartor Resartus* that "thought without reverence is barren, perhaps poisonous," he felt free to dislike the ghosts who met him in the printed sources on which he wholly depended.

But the Preface does not squarely examine the paradoxes involved in Strachey's double vow not only to serve truth more faithfully than the standard biographer but also to serve art. In a way, truth had been served more directly than he admitted by the compilations he despised. His sources enabled him by their very inclusiveness to carve out alternate interpretations from their ample materials without recourse to a single primary document. The same could hardly be said of his own compressed accounts. The arbitrariness of Strachey's portraiture has always been obvious, and criticism of its suppressions and exaggerations and distortions has accumulated from the start (it is summarized succinctly by Michael Holroyd in his biography of Strachey published in 1967[5]). Had Strachey been guilty of falsification as egregious as that of the Victorian hagiographer?

Strachey's insistence on a higher truth of art threatened, he would have readily admitted, the kind of veracity that admits the disorder of actuality. Harold Nicolson came to think that any biographer with a viewpoint—and no one ever had a viewpoint more decisively than Strachey—will be unable to write a "pure" biography, which presumes only to set down the facts. No biography ever written has been that pure, of course; any arrangement of the most unmanipulated facts expresses a point of view. Perhaps Strachey's "angle" had simply been assumed more openly. And an "angle" was necessary. Life at its messy work, as Henry James would observe, always offers the artist the irrelevant and redundant and even contradictory clutter that spoils the artist's story and blunts his theme. But might there still be a way of combining form and inclusiveness? We can see how the very virtues which made Strachey's biographic compositions so shapely sacrificed some indeterminateness that great novels—even James's own—have. But Strachey was not aiming for nor could he have achieved that kind of art.

The Preface to *Eminent Victorians*, so invariably quoted as the blast of doom for outmoded biography, does not deal fairly with the tradition out of which its own qualities arise. We are given notice that this is not to be another of those compositions in "two fat volumes with which it is our custom to commemorate the dead—who does not know them, with their ill-digested masses of material, their slipshod style, their tone of tedious panegyric, their lamentable lack of selection, of detachment, of design?"—as though this category had wholly constituted the English biographic mode till that moment. Strachey acknowledges that "we have had, it is true, a few masterpieces" (vii), but he does not feel obliged to name or describe them, and one can only wonder which, after Boswell and Johnson, he would be willing to list—Lockhart, Froude, Gaskell, Carlyle, Forster? In a footnote he honors one "honourable exception," Cook's *Nightingale*, to which he is admits a debt. His other principal sources—Purcell's *Manning* and Stanley's *Arnold*—are merely listed in his bibliography. Yet neither is at all contemptible. Only in the case of General Gordon did he fail to find a preceding biography with a good claim to factual reliability as well as to formal coherence.

Strachey was perfectly justified in believing that his four short biographies were literary works, unlike the memorials composed by the authors of most Victorian "Lives and Letters." Those journeyman works had, in their way, unconscious form, the form dictated by the very resolution to memorialize, by the suppressions imposed upon the facts at the biographer's disposal, though such a design of banal respectability was form at its most contemptible. But the best nineteenth-century biographies show the higher virtues of narrative art. Later on, in *Portraits in Miniature*, he would pay tribute to some of the historical and biographical writers he had studied—Froude, in particular, he would call "a brilliant writer, copious and vivid, with a picturesque imagination and a fine command of narrative [in which] the extraordinary succession of events assumes, as it flows through his pages, the thrilling lineaments of a great story"[6]—qualities Strachey certainly found in the *Carlyle*.

Even Stanley's *Arnold*, though governed by admiration, is shaped by a conception of a new kind of hero whose influence is more important than his actual life, and he is sometimes unobtrusively critical of his idol. But Purcell, however respectful his tone, actually gave Strachey the cue for the basic conflict he identifies in Manning, by no means minimizing his hero's worldliness, acknowledging and illustrating that this man with "a vivid belief in the Divine Presence" also was possessed, as he says, of "self-will, a despotic temper and love of power."[7] Purcell boasts justifiably that he has scrupulously included all the letters he secured, whatever they contained, as well as those revealing private diaries, written "under the seal" which show

Manning's agonies of self-reproach for these traits, his very doubts about his own motives which anticipate Strachey's suspicions.

Cook is very much more than a source for Strachey's "Nightingale." Despite Strachey's assertion that he has written from "a different angle," his angle is very often Cook's and even major passages are simply rewritten. Here is Cook:

The popular imagination of Miss Nightingale is of a girl of high degree who, moved by a wave of pity, forsook the pleasures of fashionable life for the horrors of the Crimean War; who went about the hospitals of Scutari with a lamp, scattering flowers of comfort and ministration; who retired at the close of the war into private life and lived thenceforth in the seclusion of an invalid's room—a seclusion varied only by good deeds to hospitals and nurses and by gracious and sentimental pieties . . . . The legend was fixed by Longfellow's poem and Miss Yonge's *Golden Deeds*. Its growth was favoured by the fact of Miss Nightingale's seclusion, by the hidden, almost secretive manner in which she worked, by her shrinking from publicity, by her extreme reticence about herself. It is only now, when her Papers are accessible, that her real life can be known. There are some elements of truth in the popular legend, but it is so remote from the whole truth as to convey in general impression everything but the truth. The real Florence Nightingale was very different from the legendary, but also greater. Her life was built on larger lines, her work had more importance, than belong to the legend.[8]

And here is Strachey's opening:

Everyone knows the popular conception of Florence Nightingale. The saintly, self-sacrificing woman, the delicate maiden of high degree who threw aside the pleasures of a life of ease to succour the afflicted, the Lady with the Lamp, gliding through the horrors of the hospital at Scutari, and consecrating with the radiance of her goodness the dying soldier's couch—the vision is familiar to all. But the truth was different. The Miss Nightingale of fact was not as facile fancy painted her. She worked in another fashion, and towards another end; she moved under the stress of an impetus which finds no place in the popular imagination. (135)

Strachey will not, like Cook, go on to praise the unknown Nightingale, for his next sentence is, "A Demon possessed her." Yet his reversal of romantic legend is derived from Cook, who declares that "in the real Miss Nightingale there was more that was interesting than in the legendary one." Cook does not fail to note, wryly, the politician's guile and unsentimental toughness that assisted Nightingale's endeavors—a viewpoint very close to Strachey's. "Strength of head," he says, "was quite as marked in her as goodness of heart, and she had at least as much of adroitness as of simplicity about her. Her character was in fact curiously many-sided . . . by her acts, her methods, her ways of looking at things and people—[she] is a very different person from Santa Filomena. She deserves the canonization, but not entirely for popular reasons."[9]

Cook's dryness and slight irony cannot, however, reach the level of parody that similar language conveys in Strachey's imitation. Here, as elsewhere in *Eminent Victorians*, language has an invisible source which is held up to ridicule. "Popular conception" is responsible for the clichés which the reader may mistakenly attribute to Strachey's own failure of original expression. Though Cook also is sceptical of hagiographical platitude, he does not sustain a parodistic tone.

Of course, Strachey never intended to emulate the scope of his sources. If he respected Cook's *Nightingale*, he noted that it had been composed not only from a different angle but "on a very different scale" from his own 66 pages. But the short biographical essay was hardly his discovery either. There was Johnson's *Life of Savage* and *Lives of the Poets* to refute his assertion that the English had never had their "Fontenelles and Condorcets, with their incomparable *éloges*, compressing into a few shining pages the manifold existences of men" (vi). The reader of the Preface to *Eminent Victorians* is asked to appreciate as though for the first time the "brevity which excludes everything that is redundant and nothing that is significant" (vii). In fact, collections of "worthies" and "brief lives" had had a conspicuous continuity at least since Thomas Fuller and John Aubrey (whom Strachey also praises in *Portraits in Miniature*). Plutarch influenced not only Johnson but the

nineteenth-century life-writers by providing, in addition to a
model of moral illustration congenial to the Victorian temper, a
way of summarizing personal history. The idea of the
biographical dictionary had come over from France and
culminated in such projects as Leslie Stephen's *Dictionary of
National Biography* and the English Men of Letters series of little
books written by other men of letters.

Brevity made selectivity only the more severe and arbitrary.
The propensity to suppress even major events in favor of some
selected incident deemed revelatory was promoted by the
concise, essayistic design of Strachey's profiles. He took the
artist's and the psychologist's privilege of finding symbol or
portent in small things—and the reader was free to suspect that
he had attributed special meaning to something really trivial.
Eminent Victorians contains many "aha!"s not literally justified in
his best sources though occasionally uttered by the careless
popularizer.

Because Strachey believed that character manifests itself in
life's earliest stages, Florence Nightingale, even in the nursery,
is seen by him to be already ministering, obsessively, to
suffering: "Why, as a child in the nursery when her sister had
shown a healthy pleasure in tearing her doll to pieces, had *she*
shown an almost morbid one in sewing them up again? Why
was she driven . . . to put her dog's wounded paw into elaborate
splints as if it was a human being?" (136). These touching
instances of incipient vocation are noted by Cook with the
warning:

> It is a natural temptation of biographers to give a formal
> unity to their subject by representing the child as in all
> things the father of the man; to date the vocation of their
> hero or heroine very early in life; to magnify some childish
> incident as prophetic of what is to come thereafter. . . . It has
> been recorded that she used to nurse and bandage the dolls
> which her elder sister damaged. Every book about the heroine
> of the Crimea contains, too, a tale of "first aid to the wounded"
> which Florence administered to Cap, the shepherd's collie,
> whom she found with a broken leg on the downs near
> Embley. [But] Florence Nightingale is not the only little girl
> who has been fond of nursing sick dolls or mending them
> when broken. Other children have tended wounded animals.[10]

Similarly, Strachey tells how Manning, as a schoolboy, had quick-wittedly fled, when caught "out of bounds," by jumping on a Master's horse, "giving proof of a certain dexterity of conduct which deserved to be remembered. . . . The astute youth outran the master, fetched a circle, reached the gate, jumped on to the horse's back, and rode off. For this he was properly chastised; but of what use was the chastisement? No whipping, however severe, could have eradicated from little Henry's mind a quality at least as firmly planted in it as his fear of Hell and his belief in the arguments of Paley" (7). Purcell relates the story rather differently, as told in later years by Manning's companion (unmentioned by Strachey) in the escapade. There had been no horse and the boys had *not* been caught and punished; but, more important, Purcell does not see anything more in the episode than boyish high-spirits. He offers it as demonstration of the *ordinariness* which Strachey reluctantly acknowledges to have been the general character of Manning's childhood.

The impulse toward form takes Strachey even further, however, when scenes are supplied to provide dramatic coherence, though there is little or no warrant for them in the record. Manning's conversion is the chief weak point in Strachey's portrayal of him as the absolute opportunist, for there seems every reason to suppose that a position of power and influence was available to him in the Church of England and no reason to suspect his religious conviction. But Strachey needed an occasion in which heavenly and worldly prospects were visibly confounded. As F. A. Simpson pointed out in 1944,[11] Strachey practically invented the temptation scene in Rome when the Pope is guessed to have said ("It is easy to imagine the persuasive innocence of his Italian voice," Strachey remarks), "Ah, dear Signor Manning, why don't you come over to us? Do you suppose that we should not look after you?" (60). No hint of such a conversation occurs in Strachey's only source. Purcell may have encouraged speculation by observing that Manning's diary omits any immediate record of Manning's private audience with Pius IX beyond the bald notation, "Audience to-day at the Vatican." But this biographer is content to settle for the more plausible explanation that Manning preferred to pass over in silence the Pope's ignorant allusions to the Anglican Church, which he did record in his journal later on and even relate directly to Purcell.[12]

A similar desire for dramatic climax seems to have operated

in Strachey's vision of Nightingale's cruel reproach to the dying
Sidney Herbert, her devoted collaborator. A comparison with
Cook's account shows how Strachey has both appropriated and
rewritten the whole event. Cook wrote that Nightingale "urged
her friend to 'one fight more, the best and the last' "[13] in the
struggle to reform the War Office in 1861. He does *not* give
those words to Nightingale, as Strachey does (making her quote
"Prospice" three years before Browning published it)—an error
picked up by the recent biographer, Cecil Woodham-Smith.[14]
When Herbert's sinking health made it impossible for him to
carry on, Nightingale wrote to Sir John McNeill, "What strikes
me in this great defeat more painfully even than the loss to the
Army is the triumph of the bureaucracy over the leaders—the
political aristocracy who at least advocate higher principles. A
Sidney Herbert beaten by a Ben Hawes is a greater humiliation
really (as a matter of principle) than the disaster of Scutari."[15]
In a letter of the time to Harriet Martineau she related her final
conversation with Herbert. She had, unreproachfully, compared
Herbert's collapse to the recent death of Cavour and said that
in both cases "a noble game" was tragically lost with all the
winning cards in hand. These reflections on the contest between
politicians and reformers contain, really, no personal accusation
against Herbert, but Strachey has her shrill at him, "Beaten!
Can't you see that you've simply thrown away the game? And
with the winning cards in our hands! And so noble a game!
Sidney Herbert beaten! And beaten by Ben Hawes!" And then,
says Strachey, "her full rage burst out at last," and she told
him, "It is a worse disgrace than the hospitals at Scutari," after
which the sick man "dragged himself away from her" (186) to
die. One may say that she was insensitive to speak frankly,
even without blaming him, to Herbert, and she later reproached
herself, telling Miss Martineau, "I was too hard upon him."
Rosalind Nash, who assisted Cook in writing the biography and
later revised it, has commented, however, that Strachey, in
pursuit of melodrama, missed a more delicate scene which a
different artist would have appreciated. "The real pain and
sadness of this last interview [Strachey] does not see. It is too
quiet for him. Instead we are given his two special creations,
'raging' and 'quivering' at each other."[16]
    But Strachey's artistic persona was hardly so diffident. His
was an art of bold overemphasis in which distortion played its

necessary part. Perhaps too much has been said, after all, about
the liberties taken by this fictionist whose characters were all
what E. M. Forster would have called "flat" rather than
"round"—having a fixed outline with no subtleties or changes.
His original title for his book had been "Victorian Silhouettes."
He excels particularly in minor characters who—as in Dickens—
can receive such treatment even when we demand a view of the
central character as a person having more than one or two
traits. How effectively comic are the caricatures in Strachey's
long gallery—Newman, Herbert, Gladstone, Lord Panmure,
Lord Hartington, Lord Cromer, Hurrell Froude, W. G. Ward,
A. H. Clough, Dr. Pusey, Cardinal Wiseman, General Simpson,
Benjamin Hawes, Benjamin Jowett, and others! We cease to
care that they are not literally "true." We may even not care
that the writer has not been "fair" to his principals.

Symbolism, which is a method of extreme compression, a
way of implying much by a single image, is a favorite recourse
of Stracheyan style. Any of his personages may be reduced in a
moment to the status of actors in an animal fable. Gladstone is
a serpent. Lord Acton is a fluttering moth while Manning is a
spider (and Mr. Odo Russell "a fly buzzing in gossamer," 103).
Manning is also a stormy petrel. And he is an eagle, while
Newman is a dove. Nightingale is also an eagle as well as a
swan; she is a tigress while Herbert is a stag, and Lord Panmure
is a bison. Herbert becomes the hunted stag finally destroyed
by the merciless predator: "One has the image of those wide
eyes fascinated suddenly by something feline, something strong;
there is a pause; and then the tigress has her claws in the
quivering haunches; and then—" (173). In a comparable
passage Strachey comments on Manning's campaign (as he
suspects it) against Newman: "It was the meeting of the eagle
and the dove; there was a hovering, a swoop, and then the
quick beak and the relentless talons did their work" (87). Here,
too, Strachey consciously simplified, and when Augustine Birrell
wrote to him, "Anyone less than a dove than J. H. N. would be
hard to picture," Strachey admitted, "I think perhaps my whole
treatment of Newman is over-sentimentalized—to make a foil
for the other Cardinal."[17]

As this admission shows, Strachey's distortions of
characterization also arise from another technique of
simplification, his reliance on foils or the use of one character to

set off another by sharpest contrast. A romantic passage proposes to our imagination the image of Sidney Herbert, "well born, handsome, rich, the master of Wilton—one of those great country houses, clothed with the glamour of a historic past, which are the peculiar glory of England—he possessed, besides all these advantages, so charming, so lively, so gentle a disposition, that no one who had once come near him could ever be his enemy" (170–171). Religiously sincere, idealistically motivated, he was also passive in contrast with the fierce, aggressive woman who had entrained him in her campaigns. Cook makes their opposite qualities the secret of their successful alliance, but Strachey makes their opposition destructive.

In the interest of contrast he makes Newman as absolutely different as possible from the worldly, shrewd and prosaic Manning. He depicts Newman as a sensitive man of faith, "of imagination all compact," who could literally believe in the liquification of St. Januarius' blood in Naples and whose gifts were primarily artistic, as the *Apologia* showed. Curiously, he actually diminishes the contrast, however, in altering facts. He represents Newman on a visit to his old parish as having wept at the frustration (by Manning's machinations) of his hopes for an Oxford oratory—so suggesting that he had some ambitious cravings of his own. It seems clear, in Strachey's source, Wilfrid Ward's biography of Newman, that Newman, if he wept at all, was simply moved on this occasion by recollection of his earliest beginnings as a priest.

Such crude schematic contrasts have a function. They serve to suggest that Victorian religiosity could manifest itself in sincerity as well as hypocrisy. That there is no such opposing representative of virtue in the "Arnold" essay seems to emphasize to the point of paranoia Strachey's one-sidedness about Victorian moralism. The "Arnold" is often thought to be the most unfair of the four portraits but it probably takes fewer liberties, aside from some trivial jokes about Arnold's tastes and appearance, than is ordinarily supposed. What arouses distrust is simply one's impression that Strachey's loathing for Arnold's legacy to English life was total. Not only was Arnold contemptible, but so were his protégés, those sixth-formers of a special susceptibility to the Master's influence, like Arthur Hugh Clough, about whom Strachey is more cruelly derisive, for some reason, than he is about almost anyone else in the entire book—pinning him down with ridicule not only in this but in the Nightingale essay as well. Nothing good, Strachey implies, could come out of the Rugby system, a view denied not only by Arnold's famous son in "Rugby Chapel," but by many others, like his distinguished biographer, Dean Stanley, who passed under Arnold's influence.

A more complete success occurs in "General Gordon" where a series of political caricatures sets in relief the character of the central figure. If Gordon, in his fanatic and ultimately self-destructive quest for heroic martyrdom, was a version of obsessive Victorian ambition, the politicians opposing Gordon offered a display of different ways of reaching and holding power. Gladstone, Sir Evelyn Baring and Lord Hartington are offered in splendid vignettes, brief "characters," in which Strachey's style is at its very best, enclosed within the larger frame of biographic description. We see in Gladstone an enigma, a "chimera," complex yet simple-minded in his egoism, the man "whose whole life had been devoted to the application of high principles to the affairs of State," who can also be perceived as a hypocrite and demagogue, "a crafty manipulator of men and things for the purposes of his own ambition" (307). We are shown the steely, insidious Baring, "cautious, measured, unimpeachably correct." Lord Hartington, "who was never self-seeking, who was never excited, and who had no imagination at all" (323), who was above all "slow," is indeed Gordon's opposite, his slowness the final cause of Gordon's triumphant disaster, yet he is a figure of English integrity as impressive as Gordon's. Though there has been criticism of the historic accuracy of these portraits, they are dramatically vivid in their representation of Gordon's ultimate antagonists and destroyers, the forces in Victorian society which would, paradoxically, make his apotheosis inevitable.

Corresponding to his technique in characterization is Strachey's use of the "telling detail" of description, whether invented or not. There is the "little winding stair" in the Vatican up which, we are repeatedly reminded, Manning would go on his way to see his supporter, Monsignor Talbot, and the "shaded chamber" to which Miss Nightingale retired in her later years (by all reports she remained—as Strachey, in fact, describes her—a devotee of wide-open windows and sunlight). Such architectural details have, clearly, their suggestive function.

Gesture and personal appearance play a similar role. There is the recurring glimpse in the Nightingale essay and again in the Arnold essay of poor Clough tying up parcels for Nightingale— whatever else of a more dignified order he might have done in her service. The young Clough is described in the "Arnold" as "this earnest adolescent, with the weak ankles," though there seems no evidence that he had weak ankles—he actually became an athlete. More famous is Strachey's remark that Dr. Arnold's legs were "shorter than they should have been," a bit of mischievous invention, as Strachey, whose own legs were exceptionally long, later admitted. Above all, there was General Gordon's drinking, described by Strachey. It aroused a storm of heated protest, for how could a national hero be depicted as a drunkard who had been observed to seclude himself in his tent while an attack on his camp was going on, "seated at a table, upon which were an open Bible and an open bottle of brandy" (265). Strachey got the hint for this scene from the least reliable of his sources. Such details function frequently to create that sudden collapse of attitude which corresponds to the method of bathos in sentences that derive from the model of Pope—as in the reference, already noted, to Clough's weak ankles, "This earnest adolescent with the weak ankles and the solemn face, lived entirely with the highest ends in view" (235), and as in the following: "He was obsessed by the ideals of saintliness, and convinced of the supreme importance of not eating too much" (14), or, "She sought consolation in the writings of the Mystics and in a correspondence with Mr. Jowett" (196).

Whatever their literal truth, these touches have a patent symbolic value. Sometimes the success of the method justifies Strachey's hope of striking at a higher truth than the literal. To consider Strachey's description of Gordon's drinking because it has seemed most gratuitous: "The End of General Gordon" is unified in a powerful way by Strachey's vision of Gordon as a man addicted to the intoxicant of action, even of self-sacrificial action, as an antidote to the insipidity of modern life. Strachey quotes Baudelaire: "Il faut être toujours ivre. . . . Pour ne pas sentir l'horrible fardeau du temps qui brise vos épaules et vous penche vers la terre, il faut vous enivrer sans trêve" (298). Gordon's supposititious liking for strong drink becomes a representation of his need for a spiritual inebriation; far from suggesting a cowardly retreat from duty, it is meant to signify an addiction more irresistible and dangerous than brandy, an exalted fatalism—which was the temptation concealed beneath his religiosity and sense of military duty. Strachey imagines Gordon at Khartoum saying, "Rum? Brandy? The true drunkenness lay elsewhere" (298–299). It does not matter that Gordon never said anything of the sort. It is doubtful that Gordon ever read Baudelaire.

Most of the time, as when he reduces human beings to the population of a menagerie, Strachey is essentially a comic artist, and the tragic vibration felt in "Gordon" is rarer in the other sections. This can be easily seen if one compares, as Edgar Johnson did some years ago, his portrait of Manning with Cavendish's sixteenth-century biography of Cardinal Wolsey. There is drama and spectacle in Cavendish's account but his tone is grave, the spectacle is meant to exhibit the tragic fall of gorgeous pride and lust and greed in the court of Henry VIII. His story differs from Strachey's narrative of his cardinal not merely because it ends with disgrace and execution while the modern man dies in worldly triumph and the odor of sanctity. Wolsey's own final statement, "If I had served God as diligently as I have done the king, he would not have given me over in my grey hairs,"[18] is the moral towards which Cavendish's story drives. No such intention animates Strachey's narrative. He feels only derision at self-deceiving piety masking ambition.

One asks, inevitably, whether Strachey had a sense of history, and the answer may seem to be that he was too exclusively interested in the internal contradictions of his central figures— perhaps getting some idea of Freud from his brother James—to consider fully the effect of historical forces on individual behavior. He underrates the force of abstract ideas, also, failing especially to appreciate the importance of religious controversies which meant so much to the Victorians and were not merely disguises for their baser motives. Because he cannot, himself, take religion seriously, he only intermittently respects the anguish that his four ambitious but self-reproaching Victorians feel. Though he follows Purcell in showing a man who *knew* that "for him at least the most subtle and terrible of all temptations was the temptation of worldly success" (45), and quotes from Manning's diary, he cannot help implying a conscious hypocrisy. He also expects religious feeling when none was expected by

Manning's contemporary world. He says of Manning's decision
to become a priest: "He entered the Colonial office as a
supernumerary clerk, and it was only when the offer of a
Merton Fellowship seemed to depend upon his taking orders
that his heavenly ambitions began to assume a definite shape"
(9). But Purcell makes it clear that "heavenly ambitions" were
not pretended in what was, at that time, a perfunctory
qualification for a career like any other: "In those days the fact
of taking Orders did not of necessity imply what is understood
in the Catholic Church as a vocation to ecclesiastic life. The
Church, like the Bar, or the army or navy, was one of the
recognised professions to which on leaving the University a
young man, even though of no great promise, has a right to
look as a convenient opening into active life."[19] Manning's
serious religious commitment was made later.

But Manning's attraction to the Oxford Movement does not
seem to Strachey to have had much to do with doctrine or
religious inspiration, though he acknowledges the Apocalyptic
visionary element that had been present in him ever since, as a
child, he had hidden under a table to escape the eye of God.
Thinking, perhaps, of the famous scene in *A Portrait of the Artist
as a Young Man* (just published in 1916) in which Stephen is
"tempted" by his Jesuit teacher to find attraction in the powers
of a Catholic priest—Strachey writes: "The Movement . . .
imputed an extraordinary, a transcendent merit to the profession
which Manning himself pursued . . . . It was a relief to find,
when one had supposed that one was nothing but a clergyman,
that one might, after all, be something else—one might be a
priest" (25). Such a reflection is nowhere confirmed in
Manning's actual confessions, frank as these were. Manning's
conversion, finally, is seen by Strachey as precipitated by his
perception of "the illimitable pretensions of the humblest priest
of Rome" (59) as well as by expectations of advancement. To
the expressions of self-doubt about his ambitious hopes, which
Strachey quotes from Purcell, are added the observation: "So
Manning wrote, and thought and prayed; but what are words,
and thoughts, and even prayers, to the mysterious and relentless
powers of circumstances and character?" (72).

Strachey's summary of the Oxford Movement in the second
section of "Manning" is flagrantly unserious. One can imagine
how it must have given pleasure to Bloomsbury's descendants

of the "square-toed Evangelicals who were earnest over the
atonement, confessed to a personal love of Jesus Christ, and
seemed to have arranged the whole of their lives down to the
minutest details of act and speech, with reference to Eternity"
(12). The principal actors, as Cambridge saw Oxford, were
ridiculous. John Keble, "had a thorough knowledge of the
contents of the Prayer-book, the ways of a Common Room, the
conjugations of the Greek Irregular Verbs, and the small jests
of a country parsonage; and the defects of his experience in
other directions were replaced by a zeal and a piety which
were soon to prove themselves equal, and more than equal, to
whatever calls might be made upon them." In the case of
Hurrell Froude, "the sort of ardour which impels more normal
youths to haunt Music Halls and fall in love with actresses took
the form . . . of a romantic devotion to the Deity and an intense
interest in his own soul, [and, as already noted] he was obsessed
by the ideals of saintliness, and convinced of the supreme
importance of not eating too much." Newman is treated more
respectfully, but Strachey cannot stomach his belief in miracles:
"When Newman was a child he 'wished that he could believe
the Arabian Nights were true.' When he came to be a man, his
wish seems to have been granted" (36). And so, Newman
finally took the step which ended the Movement, and "his eyes
would rest no more upon the snapdragons of Trinity." As for
the University, it "breathed such a sigh of relief as usually
follows the difficult expulsion of a hard piece of matter from a
living organism, and actually began to attend to education"
(41).

And yet, Strachey had historic intuition after all. It was his
intention to illustrate, if not explain, by his "haphazard visions,"
what he believed to be "the truth about the Victorian Age,"
and he perceives a surprising measure of historic truth. He was
often right about his subjects. He went beyond his sources
without exact warrant, but modern research sometimes has
confirmed his suspicions. He felt that one of the most detestable
aspects of the Arnold heritage was its retention, even
rationalization, of the old practice of corporal punishment and
the brutalization made possible by fagging, the absolute power
put into the hands of the senior boys at Rugby. In the tradition
practiced by the public schools before Arnold, as Strachey
noted, "the savage ritual of the whipping-block would remind a

batch of whimpering children that, though sins against man and God might be forgiven them, a false quantity could only be expiated in tears and blood" (211). But how did Arnold alter this aspect? "When Dr. Arnold considered that a flogging was necessary, he administered it with gravity. For he had no theoretical objection to corporal punishment. On the contrary, he supported it, as was his wont, by an appeal to general principles. . . . Dr. Arnold did not apply this doctrine to the Praepostors; but the boys of the lower parts of the school felt its benefits with a double force. The younger children, scourged both by Arnold and by the elder children, were given every opportunity of acquiring the simplicity, sobriety, and humbleness of mind, which are the best ornaments of youth" (219).

Strachey's sarcasm announces his distrust of Stanley's account, which minimizes the continued prominence of physical brutality in the Rugby system and even offers a justification of it by Arnold in words quoted by Stanley, imitated mockingly by Strachey: "At an age when it is almost impossible to find a true manly sense of the degradation of guilt or faults, where is the wisdom of encouraging a fantastic sense of the degradation of personal correction? What can be more false, or more adverse to the simplicity, sobriety, and humbleness of mind, which are the best ornament of youth, and the best promise of a noble manhood?"[20] Stanley, a brilliant child who had been placed in the Fourth Form on entrance and promoted to the Fifth six months later, had been almost exempt from the bullying of the older boys. He became the Master's favorite very promptly, and even before graduation was one of the little corps of the elite who would defend Arnold against his critics in the outside world, many of whom were only prejudiced against Arnold because of his anti-Tory political views. In his biography, therefore, he deals evasively with the feature of Rugby which was a principal weapon in the hands of Arnold's detractors.

He thus does not mention the many cases in which flogging by the Praepostors was unquestioningly supported by Arnold. In 1832, for example, one of the lower boys, Nicholas Marshall, defied some of the prefects who were attempting to cane him for a minor infraction, seizing the leaded cane itself from their hands and breaking it in two, and running off. The boy was expelled and the father who came to complain was shown the door by Arnold. But a more striking omission is an instance of unjustified brutality by Arnold himself in that same year. Making his rounds through the lower forms, Arnold asked a child named March to construe a passage in Xenophon. The boy told the Doctor that this point in the book had not been reached, which seemed contradicted by the notes of the Assistant Master. Arnold, in a rage at what he considered the most heinous of crimes, blatant lying, personally flogged March—a child of delicate health—with eighteen furious blows. It turned out that the boy had been right, and Arnold not only hastily brutal but mistaken in his accusation, and the case was much publicized by the press.[21] Stanley does not mention either of these or any other of the cases in which Arnold's rod was exerted against "the wickedness of young boys"—and neither does Strachey, consequently, though he clearly assumes the worst.

Similarly, Strachey pressed Cook's balanced portrait of Nightingale beyond the overt evidence, sometimes distorting the facts; but his intuition may be justified, after all, when he makes use of Cook's detached observations to show her as an obsessive egotist and hints at a pathology of narcissism and manipulativeness. Most biographers since Cook—like Cecil Woodham-Smith—have simply based their accounts on Cook's basic research, and Strachey, of course, never looked at a document; he had only his intuitions. But the most recent study of the voluminous unpublished Nightingale materials shows that Cook could have presented a record that might have gone much further in justifying Strachey's indictment.[22] F. B. Smith has recently written a startling revisionist biography full of new facts without denying—as Strachey did not deny either—the importance of Nightingale's achievements. This new story is one of self-serving intrigue from the start of Nightingale's career in the Crimea through her campaign for the reform of the Army medical services and the sanitary conditions of Army barracks, and then for "sanitary reform" in India, and finally in the course of her establishment of nursing standards and training. Smith's book exposes the fallacy that doers of good must themselves be good persons, which Strachey, though possessed of incomplete evidence in Nightingale's case, doubted on principle.

One may note, by way of example, a few of the new insights we now possess into the character that made her famous, that of the Lady with the Lamp at Scutari. Strachey passes over uncritically, taking his cue from Cook, Nightingale's year as superintendent of a charitable London nursing home just before the outbreak of the Crimean War; Smith shows that already she displayed a talent for dominating her associates and opponents, claiming success for improvements not due to her and managing to put on others the blame for failures of her own. Her Crimean service was marked by a degree of careerism unsuspected till Smith's book appeared. Even the "coincidence" in which Sidney Herbert's letter inviting her services and hers offering them to the War Office crossed in the mail—which Strachey accepts unquestioningly—turns out to be simply a charming story; it appears that she had already used her influence in high places and arranged for the invitation, which was only a formal confirmation. Once launched, she made sure that she had no rivals in the field, though there were a number of others with more substantial claims to competence and experience in the management of hospitals and nurses. Indifferent to formal religious conformity herself, she used the Protestant nervousness of the times to raise doubts about the leaders of various groups of Catholic Sisters of Mercy and some leaders and nursing volunteers with "Puseyite" affiliations; it seems that she instigated, even drafted, the documents which secured from Sidney Herbert official notification of her headship. Later, she actually kept some of these nurses from joining the 40 who were nursing 3,000 sick men under her direction, claiming that more would "get under our feet." Obscured by her and her previous biographers has been the fact that most of the nursing was still done by male orderlies.

Though she generally preferred to make her moves seem the free initiative of others, she also later claimed credit where she did not deserve it; it appears that she did not, as she let it be known, pay for the rebuilding of the Scutari hospital out of her own pocket; payment came entirely from the government and a fund raised by the London *Times*. Nor was she effective in the direction of the nurses and nuns enrolled under her; there was mutiny and complaint among them. What she did do well, it appears, is conduct a voluminous correspondence. Some of these were letters of condolence to the widows of patients who died; others were orders, complaints and insinuations to her supporters in England, which organized a propaganda network that kept her in power.

Florence Nightingale's achievements at Scutari were considerable and it even can be argued that the less attractive qualities of her character—her skill at underhanded influence, her agglomeration of personal power, even her deceptions—forwarded the work she did there when confronted with revolting disorder and the indifference of the Army. But the myth of the saintly, gentle Lady with the Lamp soon displayed in the press—particularly by reports published in the *Times* by several correspondents and by A. W. Kinglake, the historian—had a political function. As Smith says, they "created the Lady with the Lamp as the living counter to the muddle and national shame of war that failed public expectations of early glory. . . . She became a neutral, safely non-political diversionary focus for the discontents that might otherwise have been concentrated by J. A. Roebuck, Augustus Stafford, Charles Dickens and other radical critics in their attack on aristocratic dominance and mismanagement."[23]

It may be that Strachey had some suspicion of the real meaning of the Nightingale canonization—and that this historic insight fuels his antagonism for the Lady with the Lamp. Not that he did not shudder at the horrors she fought against, of course. All his loathing for the recent war is felt in his description of the spectacle of the hospital at Scutari when Nightingale first arrived there. His contempt for the callousness of Army leadership, and for politicians who support it in all wars, is felt in satiric characterizations of Nightingale's opponents like Dr. John Hall, General Simpson, Lord Panmure. But he may have understood her value to English conservatism, and her illustration, in her own personality, of the Victorian qualities he disliked.

What he overlooks in the process is another story about Florence Nightingale which might have been more visible to his feminist friend, Virginia Woolf. Without finding Nightingale a more attractive person, one may want to see more clearly the meaning of her struggle to emerge out of the confinement of the female destiny assigned to her. She had a keen sense of her own dilemma when, as a young woman, she regarded with aversion the prospect of an upper-class marriage, though it might satisfy

her "passional nature," she admitted in the case of one attractive
suitor. But her journal goes on, we read in Cook:

> I could not satisfy this nature by spending a life with him in
> making society and arranging domestic things . . . . To be
> nailed to a continuation and exaggeration of my present life,
> without hope of another, would be intolerable to me.
> Voluntarily to put it out of my power ever to be able to seize
> the chance of forming for myself a true and rich life would
> seem to me like suicide . . . . I don't agree at all that a
> woman has no reason (if she does not care for anyone else)
> for not marrying a good man who asks her. I think He has as
> clearly marked out some to be single women as He has others
> to be wives. . . . There are women of intellectual or actively
> moral natures for whom marriage (unless it reaches the
> perfect ideal) means the sacrifice of their higher capacities to
> the satisfaction of their lower. . . . Marriage . . . is often an
> initiation into the meaning of the inexorable word Never;
> which does not deprive us, it is true, of what "at their
> festivals the idle and inconsiderate call life," but which brings
> in reality the end of our lives, and the chill of death with it.[24]

That she had to find fulfillment in a society which practically
forbade women to take an active role and to try to change
things goes far to explain her intense cultivation of indirect
methods, her art of conniving. A woman in a man's world, after
all, she perfected what Smith calls her "secretarial" mode of
gaining her ends: "Secretive, purposeful, she was to satisfy
herself with manipulating persons having executive powers
whilst she remained unseen and unsung, savouring the private
knowledge of the process."[25] A pliant Sidney Herbert was
absolutely necessary to the practical efficacy of a Florence
Nightingale. But Strachey's artistic economy forbade the
introduction of too much complexity, and forbade much
sympathy for her. He will permit us to admire her achievements
but he cannot resist sneers that keep us from empathy. Our last
glimpse of her, a fat, senile old woman who had lost her hawk-
like ferocity and "indulged in sentimental friendships with
young girls" (200) sends her out of our minds with a snigger.

Strachey's historic sense is best illustrated, however, in "The
End of General Gordon." This essay is generally admired for its

dramatic brilliance and its psychological portraiture, but it should be noted that here Strachey sees with a political perceptiveness not present in any of his sources. Strachey's Gordon becomes a part of a complex political struggle. British imperialism becomes the real object of his irony rather than Gordon himself. So, we begin with Gordon's Chinese phase where, Strachey says, "though he was too late to take part in the capture of the Taku Forts, he was in time to witness the destruction of the Summer Palace at Pekin—an act by which Lord Elgin, in the name of European civilization, took vengeance upon the barbarism of the East" (248). After his own defeat of the Taiping Rebellion, "Chinese Gordon" had a "dread of the world's contaminations," and failed to take up the position in British society that his services to the Empire might have allowed, but the Empire would find use for him despite—or rather because of—his peculiar fastidiousness and his conviction that God would lead him into an appropriate expression of his taste for danger and command.

After a period of seclusion and waiting for the Divine summons, he accepts the Governorship of the Equatorial Provinces of the Sudan and struggles for six appalling years to establish order there. He then takes a higher post, the Governor-Generalship of the whole Sudan, in which he pits himself, the representative of the enlightened West, against "oriental" administrative corruption and the slave-trade. But as Strachey observes: "The Pashas were anxious to use him as a respectable mask for their own nefarious dealings; and the representatives of the European creditors, who looked upon him as an irresponsible intruder, were anxious simply to get rid of him as soon as they could" (266). Despite his military services in suppressing the power of native chiefs, he is not really trusted by the Pashas—he does not know, for example, when to accept a bribe, and his service is ended.

After another interval during which he takes on a succession of brief assignments in India, in China, in Mauritius, and thinks of going next to the Congo for the king of the Belgians, his final opportunity arrives in the assumption by Britain of the governorship of Egypt, nominally still ruled by the Pashas who were proving themselves unable to suppress insurrections. Though the British have bombed Alexandria and sent in their own soldiers, they do not yet understand fully, as Strachey says, that they are henceforth the masters of the country. Despite the increasing incompetence of the Pashas, the Liberals in parliament want to withdraw British forces from Egypt. Gladstone, the Prime Minister, inclines towards peaceful withdrawal. Others know where British interests lie and want Britain to dig in, militarily as well as economically. Public opinion has been aroused by the sacrifice of unsupported British troops to the advancing power of the chief rebel leader, the Mahdi. Khartoum is in danger of being taken by him.

It is at this point that Gordon suddenly seems to be the one man needed. In a newspaper interview he had expressed himself in favor of immediate British intervention. And immediately Lord Granville, the Foreign Secretary, whom we might call a hawk, has suggested that he be sent as an emissary to Khartoum. Sir Evelyn Baring, *de facto* ruler of Egypt as the British representative in charge of the country's economy, in the interests of its enormous debt to Britain, is reluctant, but Lord Wolsey, Adjutant General of the Forces, is in favor. Gordon will go. His instructions, however, are ambiguous; he is to assist the *evacuation* of the Sudan by the British, though his whole previous career as well as his expressed views on the immediate crisis suggest that he is only fit for an opposite course.

Strachey ponders the explanation for Gordon's appointment. Was the government yielding simply to the clamor for Gordon in the press—or was this very clamor encouraged by the war party? "The engineering of a newspaper agitation may not have been an impossibility—even so long ago as 1884" (295). The imperialists in the Cabinet, like Lord Hartington, disliked the idea of withdrawal, though this was official policy. So, what if someone like Gordon was sent out; what would happen? "Was it not possible that, once there, given his views and character, he would, for some reason or other, refrain from carrying out a pacific retreat? . . . Was it not possible that General Gordon might get into difficulties, that he might be surrounded and cut off from Egypt? If that were to happen, how could the English Government avoid the necessity of sending an expedition to rescue him? . . . In short, would not the dispatch of General Gordon to Khartoum involve, almost inevitably, the conquest of the Sudan by British troops, followed by a British occupation?"

Such speculative representation of the secret thoughts of

some of Britain's leaders has no documentary verification, of course—any more than Strachey's imagination of Manning's private conversation with Pius IX. But it has historic probability. For so it turns out—or almost. The relief expedition that finally arrived at Khartoum to find Gordon's severed head stuck in a tree on the public highway was only two days late. Anyhow, the British had a military martyr and British imperialism's course was now unstoppable. The future, as Strachey says, "lay with Major Kitchener and his Maxim-Nordenfeldt guns." Thirteen years later, "it had all ended very happily—in a glorious slaughter of twenty thousand Arabs, a vast addition to the British Empire, and a step in the Peerage for Sir Evelyn Baring" (349–350).

If the four studies are unified by any theme it is not so much the effect of religion on the Victorian personality, as is often said—though all of Strachey's subjects were religious and even felt they had a religious mission, a vocation of service to the Christian God. His subjects are linked more significantly by their common quality of being creatures possessed of a personal energy that had nothing particularly religious about it. It was the same energy that had effected all the transformations and achievements of the great nineteenth century. In the possession of it they were truly representative of the Victorian age. Strachey, the languid invalid, the pacifist, the artistic dilettante, sees this energy as demonic, however. The upward and onward thrust of men, machines and money had produced in the end the horror of the War, and he has only dread and contempt for all the strenuosity which had led society to such an end.

I have suggested earlier that there is a parodistic element in Strachey's use of his sources and we can see that the genre that he pretends stylistically to follow is that of the biographical tribute to achievement which shows how its hero has attained his eminence by the combination of innate gifts and incessant effort. There are other implied patterns that receive their due of parody, also. The four histories can be seen as Victorian Saints' Lives. Manning, Nightingale, Arnold and Gordon all saw themselves as soldiers of the faith. Arnold saw himself as a kind of prophet of moral truth to the heathen. Nightingale saw herself as suffering and sacrificing, besieged by enemies, chained to her bed of pain, striving to imitate Christ. Gordon saw himself as the foreordained martyr who waited to embrace his death with eagerness. In reading these biographies against their hagiographical or quasi-hagiographical sources we see how Strachey deliberately mocks by parodistic imitation the view of these personages which either they themselves or the age accepted.

But he also, parodistically, discloses that they were versions of those gifted and incessantly industrious, resourceful men who had risen to the top in the bustling advance of the industrial age. In many ways these careers are accounted for in the same way as the lives held up as examples to ambitious youth by Samuel Smiles in his *Lives of the Engineers* (1861) and its sequels, group biographies of successful engineers and industrialists who had been moral, inventive and above all persevering. But Strachey inverts Smiles. The energy that animates his aspiring subjects is terrifying. After parodying Nightingale as a saint according to popular conception, in the opening passage already quoted, he says, "a Demon possessed her." The demon of unresting striving is behind the "restlessness" that she showed even as a girl. "She would think of nothing but how to satisfy that singular craving of hers to be *doing* something" (137), he says, at the same time rejecting and sharing the astonishment of her family.

And so, "with amazing persistence" she managed for years to acquire education and training; while still carrying on her role as the member of an upper-class household, "she yet possessed the energy to collect the knowledge and to undergo the experience which alone would enable her to do what she had determined she would do in the end" (139). At Scutari she descended like a general manager of genius to establish order, to organize resources rationally, to "expedite," as we say, the arrival and distribution of necessary supplies "by strict method, by stern discipline, by rigid attention to detail, by ceaseless labour, by the fixed determination of an indomitable will" (156). As Cook says, "in the Crimea, it was as Administrator and Reformer, more than as Angel, that she showed her peculiar powers."[26] Her gifts were of the same kind as those that made for a successful industrial enterprise. She was tireless at her desk as she worked over her correspondence during the night while others slept. "She would fill pages with recommendations and suggestions, with criticisms of the minutest details of organization, with elaborate calculations of contingencies, with exhaustive analyses and statistical statements" (157). When she inspected the hospitals in the Crimea, "she spent whole days in the saddle, or was driven over those bleak and rocky heights in a baggage cart. Sometimes she stood for hours in a heavily falling snow, and would only reach her hut at dead of night after walking for miles through perilous ravines" (161). Only a hair—the implication of a latent mockery which is parody—separates the tone of this from praise.

On her return to England, her health was shattered, but she would not rest. "Mad—possessed—perhaps she was. A demonic frenzy had seized upon her. As she lay upon her sofa, gasping, she devoured blue-books, dictated letters, and, in the intervals of her palpitations, cracked her febrile jokes." Nightingale's real or neurotic invalidism did not hamper her. It probably promoted her industry by enabling her to economize energy, protected from interruptions and waited on by loyal helpers who were spurred to emulate her. "Let them look at her lying there pale and breathless on the couch; could it be said that she spared herself? Why, then, should she spare others?" (173). And so, she tackled the improvement of Army hospitals, published her 800-page report, directed from behind the scenes the work of the Royal Commission appointed to investigate the matter. She was told to rest, and she was furious. Then, when the immense task succeeded, she was, in Strachey's description, "still ravenous for more and more work, her activities had branched out into new directions" (183). She turned to the condition of the Army in India, she wrote her *Notes on Hospitals*, she organized a nurses' training program, she launched an effort to reform the War Office itself. Strachey's exaggeration of her effect on Sidney Herbert can be seen as a coherent part of his profile—"could it be said that she spared herself? Why, then should she spare others?"

Nightingale, as Strachey describes her, lived on to the age of ninety according to this principle, exercising influence, writing innumerable letters and reports, even a three-volume treatise to settle all the major religious questions of the ages—the Origin of Evil, Predestination and Free Will, the Future Life, the Plan of Creation. What could not be achieved with the application of enough energy? One can see why Strachey takes a wicked pleasure in visualizing her end in senile inaction and amiability.

Each of the other portraits suggests some degree of the same obsession with entrepreneurial doing that is so conspicuous in Strachey's Florence Nightingale. Manning's early exhibition of "dexterity" in school is converted, only by the parodistic tone, from a promise of good achievement to a gift for evil subterfuge. Manning's energy, like Nightingale's, is parodically praised: "Through all the changes of his fortunes the powerful spirit of the man worked on undismayed" (9). When he had reached the age of thirty-eight, he was "the rising man in the Church of England" with powerful connections in the world at large where "he busied himself with matters of such varied scope as National Education, the administration of the Poor Law, and the Employment of Women" (43). A literal athleticism seems the corollary of his energetic striving and doing; he was to be seen, says Strachey, "galloping over the downs in breeches and gaiters, or cutting brilliant figures on the ice" (44). And the same athleticism figuratively characterizes his efforts and struggles of spirit. When he just misses, in time, the temptation of a bishopric in the Anglican Church, Strachey says, "Manning's 'poor soul' had scented nobler quarry" (59). His effect upon Cardinal Wiseman is to make him undertake what he considers "a great wrestling-match with infidelity" (68).

Now, in the Catholic Church, Provost of Westminster, his energy applies itself to gaining influence, eliminating rivals, entering into controversies and stirring up the easy-going Wiseman. Strachey comments that Wiseman "had fallen into the hands of one who cared very little for the gentle pleasures of repose" (66–67). Manning "flung himself into the fray with that unyielding intensity of fervour, that passion for the extreme and absolute, which," says Strachey, only seeming, again, to applaud, is "the very life-blood of the Church of Rome" (67). Soon, he is appointed to the See of Westminster and is the supreme ruler of Roman Catholic England. "Power had come to him at last; and he seized it with all the avidity of a born autocrat" (86). At the Vatican Council to consider Papal Infallibility, he knew the ropes and used them with a "serviceable and yet discreet alacrity." And, at last, he has the Cardinal's hat. But he is not yet content; he would deny Newman the same reward, and Newman realizes that "a secret and powerful force [is] working against him" (121).

Even as an old man his energy does not flag. "He ruled his diocese with the despotic zeal of a born administrator. He threw himself into social work of every kind; he organized charities, he lectured on temperance. He delivered innumerable sermons; he produced an unending series of devotional books. . . . Nor was it only among his own community that his energy and experience found scope. He gradually came to play an important part in public affairs, upon questions of labour, poverty and education. He sat on Royal Commissions, and corresponded with Cabinet Ministers. At last, no philanthropic meeting at the Guildhall was considered complete without the presence of Cardinal Manning" (112–113). He notes in his diary: "They say I am ambitious, but do I rest in my ambition?" And Strachey answers: "No, assuredly he did not rest; but worked now with no *arrière pensée* for the greater glory of God. A kind of frenzy fell upon him. Poverty, drunkenness, vice, all the horrors and terrors of our civilization, seized upon his mind and urged him forward to new fields of action and new fields of thought" (124). And so, Death itself is forced to "struggle step by step" (128) with him like a wrestler. His last anxiety, Gladstone thought, was that he had not completed his work.

Compared to the demonic frenzy that governs Strachey's Nightingale and Manning, Arnold seems a less active figure. He even is said to have suffered from the handicap of a dislike of early rising, though he struggled against it with true Victorian resolution. (Interestingly, Nightingale's early diaries contain confessions of the same youthful weakness!) Yet everything about his appearance denoted "energy, earnestness, and the best intentions" (210), the first quality linking him to the more visibly active achievers. In his application to the task of creating a powerful instrument of educational influence, he never ceased to labor. Not only within Rugby but outside it he made himself felt, and he published seventeen volumes of learned studies, aside from his numerous pamphlets and articles on current questions, Strachey points out. Carlyle, after visiting Rugby, characterized Arnold as "a man of unhasting, unresting diligence" (230). Mrs. Arnold, who bore him six children during the first eight years of marriage, and then four more, would, Strachey jokes, have no doubt agreed.

In his emphasis on achievement through influence, Strachey, once more, parodistically reverses his source, for Stanley's "Arnold" has exactly for its object the celebration of Arnold's importance as a man whose main accomplishment became visible in others. But the influence which produced Stanley himself and compelled his reverence seems malign to Strachey who had felt it at Abbotsholme School where all the Arnoldian Rugby features prevailed—the high importance of organized athletics (no longer the schoolboy's free escape from authority), the system which made deputy bullies of the senior boys, the medieval disinterest in modern fields of knowledge, and the religiosity which fortified the Master's absolute tyranny. The public school ethos had created a ruling class in whom the traits of competitiveness and aggression, esteemed in Victorian biography, had led to the hateful War.

It was in the final essay on Gordon, however, that Strachey came most profoundly to terms with the Victorian exaltation of action which leads ultimately to the battlefield, to wanton slaughter in the name of dubious causes. Strachey presents Gordon at the outset during a moment of enforced retirement in 1883 when "it might have seemed that a life of inordinate activity had found at last a longed-for, a final peacefulness" (246). Nothing, of course, could have been less true. Gordon was the sword in the scabbard; he lived waiting for the moment when he would again be called to his true purpose. "And it was not in peace and rest, but in ruin and horror, that he reached his end" (246).

Gordon's skills as a military commander are reminiscent, also, of Smiles' engineers. Undertaking to defeat the Taiping rebellion in 1863, he organized with systematic efficiency the military clean-up of an area of 14,000 square miles and a population of twenty million. In the Sudan he worked in the same way "to suppress insurrections, make roads, establish fortified posts, and enforce the government monopoly of ivory" (263) during "six years of extraordinary, desperate, unceasing, and ungrateful labour" (261). In between there had been a period of quiet when he seemed destined to be a hermit. But he was "no simple quietist. He was an English gentleman, an officer, a man of energy and action, a lover of danger and the audacities that defeat danger, a passionate creature, flowing over with the self-assertiveness of independent judgement and the arbitrary temper of command" (259). The pious visionary of Gravesend was to be "the restless hero of three continents." The next three years proved "the most *mouvementés*" of his life, and then he created for himself a supreme demonstration of the value of action. It is correct to say that he created it for himself, out of his own impulsion towards a heroic destiny, even though, as noticed above, he was manipulated to his final scene by politicians. A self-reproacher like the other eminent Victorians, he could question his motives for holding out at Khartoum when he was surrounded by the forces of the Mahdi: "I believe ambition put me here in this ruin" (305). His personal ambition was nothing less than the ambition to be an English Leonidas. Do-or-die heroism had its uses for British imperialism even though, as in Florence Nightingale's War, it became clear that "someone had blundered." Such heroics were an ultimate expression of the will to action exercised even at the price of the actor's personal life.

In describing his four Victorians in this way, Strachey does not completely reverse the tradition of praise in the biographical mode he rejected. He makes us feel the remarkableness of each of his four subjects. In the end, we do not admire them, and yet we have to concede their justifiable "eminence." With the possible exception of Arnold, they remain imposing. This complexity of attitude has been rarely achieved by Strachey's imitators. It has not even been sufficiently noted by Strachey's own fine biographer, who declares that though the Preface to *Eminent Victorians* asserted the importance of the individual, "the essays that followed exemplified only the vanity and littleness of the self-important." Strachey's portraits, says Holroyd, stress "villainy masquerading as virtue,"[27] and that is all. But the secret sympathy which would surface as a sentimental indulgence in *Queen Victoria* operates in this earlier and finer work to maintain an unwilling respect for his subjects. Rampant egotists though his Victorians are, they are not little and not conscious villains. Their terrifying energies are devoted to ends they consider ideal, and they are as curiously awe-inspiring as they are self-serving.

CHAPTER FOUR

A. J. A. Symons'
The Quest for Corvo

A. O. J. COCKSHUT

I

At first sight, Frederick Rolfe (Baron Corvo) appears to belong to a distinguished class of English writers who, while unknown or little known in their lifetime, acquired posthumous fame. Traherne and Hopkins, for instance, each provide the English literary tradition with works of genius that are unique. If either were blotted out, we should know at once that there could be no substitute. As William Gerard Hamilton said: "Johnson is dead. Let us go to the next best. There is nobody." And indeed, the growth of Rolfe's reputation was slow. He died in 1913. Osbert Sitwell, an avid reader of avant-garde literature and, for a time, a fellow-resident in Venice, did not hear of him till 1919.[1] Shane Leslie and others founded the Corvine Society in 1929; A. J. A. Symons began to enquire about his life in 1925, and eventually published *The Quest for Corvo* in 1934. Many of Rolfe's works were published posthumously, some more than twenty years after his death.

But a few moments' reflection will be enough to convince us that Rolfe is not comparable to Traherne and Hopkins. He is essentially a cult figure, a lover of long, unknown (or often non-existent) barbarously-formed words; a pseudo-scholar, who was, except for a few pieces of specialized knowledge, very ignorant; a dandy; and a specialist in vituperation. That he wrote in the end only about himself need not have disqualified him for greatness. Some of the world's greatest books are autobiographies. Rolfe was no autobiographer, but rather a fantasist of egoism. We are not surprised when we read that he could paint his own face more than a hundred times in a professedly historical picture. It would be unfair to say that his literary appeal is confined to dandies like himself. Some of his admirers, like Shane Leslie, have been sensible and gifted people. But probably he has appealed to some odd corner of the personality, some spirit of holiday from the real world. In serious and sensible people, an admiration for Rolfe is not as a rule meant seriously. He appeals in the main to dandies, or to those who are interested, as scholars, in dandyism, or to connoisseurs of vituperation. And yet, there remains a widespread feeling, that, in Osbert Sitwell's words, "He was most assuredly not banal."[2]

II

Symons' book occupies an interesting and in some ways peculiar place in the history of biographic art. The basic Victorian model[3] continued substantially unchanged for longer than is perhaps generally supposed. Leonard Huxley's life of his father, T. H. Huxley (1900) conforms no more closely to the tradition than does Lord Ronaldshay's life of Curzon (1928). And there are a few examples, such as G. M. Trevelyan's life of Edward Grey (1937), which are actually later than Symons' book. To summarize a complex matter briefly, we may say that the distinguishing features are close attention to milieu of family and education, reliance on letters as principal source, an admiring attitude to the subject, and a tacit acceptance that the honours accorded by the world are indications of real distinction. There is little or no interest in childhood, reticence on the subjects of sex and money, and a determination to allow the subject to tell his own story as far as he will. The extent to which Lytton Strachey, who produced his most important books between 1918 and 1921, and who was dead before Symons' work appeared, revolutionized this tradition has often been the subject of misunderstanding. He did away with the reverence, certainly. But he did hardly any research; almost every fact that is not simply a baseless speculation of Strachey's own comes from the big Victorian lives. And he is, if possible, even more reticent about sex than his predecessors had been. Like the Victorian *Punch*, he thought drink was funny, and invented a (probably false) accusation of excess about General Gordon, but he would not have dreamt of speculating on his sexual constitution. Strachey's formula is in essence the Victorian one, much shortened, and then turned upside down by the operation of Voltairean sneers. There is nothing new in Strachey's method; it is the application of French eighteenth-century wit to a time-honoured nineteenth-century English formula.

It is a curious quirk of history that the end of the anti-Victorian phase of English culture (which can be dated about 1940) led to, or at least coincided with, a break with the great and venerable Victorian tradition of writing biography. Reticence was much reduced or disappeared altogether; psychological interpretations tended to replace letters and reminiscences. Books became shorter (in that, Strachey had been a pioneer) and facts sparser. What is Symons' place in this transformation?

First we notice that the book is not a biography, but rather a proposal to write a biography. In a sense it is a partial autobiography—the autobiography of the biographer. Its time-scale records events not as they occurred but as they were speculated upon or discovered. The author becomes for the reader at least as familiar a figure as the subject; and some of those who gave him information become very vivid too. At the same time Rolfe's milieu, family, schools, literary London, Venice and the rest remain vague. Partly, no doubt, this can be attributed to Rolfe's solitary life and strangeness. But even a thoroughly conventional subject, treated by Symons' method, would remain partly out of context. The method lends itself to the intense realization of certain issues and certain moments, as they are recalled by his informants, and long, featureless gaps between these moments. The book is highly expressive at times, but only at selective times. It is like a painting in which a few figures, or rather a few features of one figure, leap to the eye, and the background is blurred. A greater contrast with the Victorian method, where we get accustomed to the reassuring presence at the top of the page of "year 1876, aet. 66" and the like, can hardly be imagined.

In several respects, Symons was skilful or fortunate in his choice of method. Its romantic unevenness imitates that of its subject; a man like Rolfe, who always seemed to set out to defeat himself, would be ill-served by the systematic and chronological scheme appropriate to books like Morley's *Gladstone*. And one or two later attempts to treat Rolfe in accordance with the old method[4] have been rather unconvincing, partly for this reason. The trouble is that their admirable zeal in discovering facts is not matched by subtlety of interpretation. Many of Rolfe's actions are deeply ambiguous; and a superficial interpretation, or the absence of any interpretation, must be felt as a serious blemish. More important, from the point of view of Symons' reputation, which rests almost entirely on this one book, his method was in harmony with a particular phase of taste. That anti-classical spirit, which preferred Constable's sketches to his works in their definitive state, which preferred a caricature by Lytton Strachey to a full portrait by Wilfrid Ward or Monypenny and Buckle—this spirit delighted in Symons' innovations.

He arrived at them, it would seem, more by good fortune and natural inclination than by any deep thought. They enabled him to write much more about himself than previous biographers had done. He enjoyed this; and he justified it by a theory which is as characteristic as it is unacceptable. In a paper read to a dining club in 1926, he had said of Rolfe: "He would have recounted his past life for hours; for, like all good talkers, his favourite subject was himself."[5] At the same time, he had a strong dislike (which might well be called ignorant and philistine) for the classic biographies of the previous century. On these he wrote: "English biography has lamentably failed. It has failed in beauty as it has in truth."[6] But his lack of any very clear understanding of his own work and its originality can be seen from his praise, in the same essay, of Lytton Strachey, whose method, as we have seen, had nothing in common with his own, and was really only a reversed continuation of the high Victorian one. It is not difficult to understand this praise. Symons was, above all, a devotee of fashion. His dandyism, his anxiety to belong to the right clubs, his whole way of life, testify to this. His talk on "Tradition in Biography" hit the fashion of 1926 exactly, at the cost of falsifying literary history. Like many bibliophiles, Symons tended to be ignorant of anything that fell outside the narrow range of his special expertise. He did know

quite a lot about the writers of the 1890s. But his generalizations
about the Victorian age are those of a schoolboy, and are not
worth quoting.

His method had yet other advantages. Some of those who
gave him information were very interesting people and they
were all utterly different from Rolfe himself. There was a great
gain in variety, a release, for which many readers will have felt
the need, from Rolfe's oppressive egoism. And then, the sense,
which the reader of *The Quest* has, of being in the 1920s and
1930s, rather than in Rolfe's own time, is valuable because it is
symbolic of the gulf in European civilization created by the war
of 1914. The book has an enchanting sense of "near and far."
On the one hand, Symons was investigating and writing when
many of Rolfe's contemporaries and seniors were still alive.
(Had Rolfe lived he would have been seventy-four in the year
The Quest was published.) On the other, the book speaks of a
vanished world. It is hardly possible to imagine Rolfe in the
post-war period. Symons does not make the mistake of
presenting him as typical of his time—Rolfe would have been a
strange and exceptional personality in any age—but he assuredly
belongs and could belong to no other.

Something must be said about Symons' accuracy. Much of
his material comes from personal reminiscence of meetings with
Rolfe's acquaintances, and cannot easily be checked. Even so,
his brother believed that some episodes were altered or
heightened with a view to dramatic effect.[7] There can be no
doubt, however, of the seriousness of his desire to discover all
he could about Rolfe, or of his assiduity in the search. He had
the mind of a bibliophile and bibliographer, rather than that of
a scholar, and he was accustomed to noting details accurately.
His inaccuracies are of a special kind, characteristic of those
who find it difficult to bridge the gap between fact and
imaginative interpretation. Symons was capable of being very
exact about details at the same time as he was being slackly
speculative about generalities. A single example will serve. In
his essay on Theodore Hook, he writes: "When Byron and Sir
Robert Peel, who were both born in 1788, dawdled at Harrow,
young Hook, of exactly equal age, dawdled also."[8] No doubt it
is quite true that Harrow, in the early years of the nineteenth
century, was not a very earnest society. Neither Byron nor
Hook was an earnest boy. But Peel! Peel was the best scholar of

his day at Oxford, and, in the opinion of many, the most industrious Prime Minister this country ever had. He must have worked at Harrow. Possibly Symons knew this; at any rate he could easily have discovered it. But he did not think of it; his imagination was so much carried away by the pleasing vision of these three celebrities being schoolboys together that he did not choose to reflect on the accuracy of his words. Of deliberate falsification we can certainly acquit him; and of carelessness, too, except in the special sense just explained. Errors in *The Quest* are similar, except where they spring from a partially defective understanding of his subject. These are, of course, much more important, and I speak of them later.

The relation of the author of a biography to his subject raises questions as interesting as they are elusive. And the questions are more interesting than usual in this case, because, as we have seen, the book is, in part, a fragment of autobiography. His brother speaks of his deep interest in the 1890s: "he professed a great admiration for Poe, for Algernon Blackwood, for the artists, poets and prose-writers of the Nineties, and in general for all artists who dealt romantically with macabre themes."[9]

He was partly drawn to Rolfe by the obscurity of the subject, the sheer difficulty of finding out anything about him; and partly by certain (rather limited) similarities of temperament. Both Rolfe and Symons were dandies, bibliophiles and calligraphers. Both were extravagant and improvident; both combined a longing for spectacular worldly success with a (probably much deeper and more concealed) fascination with failure. Symons perhaps put his finger on his deepest affinity with Rolfe when he said: "The gambler wishes always in his heart to lose."[10]

But the differences between the two were just as fundamental, or more so. Symons was worldly in a simple, naive sense in which Rolfe was not. He had no interest in religion, and though many of the people who inspired his curiosity were homosexual, he seems to have had no homosexual bent. In one most important respect, the two men were opposites. Everything Rolfe did and was seems to be motivated by pride; Symons is the perfect type of the man motivated by vanity, the man who does not know what he is, or what he wishes to become, and who sees himself reflected in the opinions of others. Symons

was close enough to Rolfe to have sympathy, and far enough
away to attempt an objective view.

And if Rolfe was unique, Symons amuses us by conforming
in so many ways to a familiar type. He is the perennial "old
young man," so familiar to generations of Oxford dons. He
said, when he was still young enough to be an undergraduate,
that he was building and shaping his life as an architect plans a
house.[11] Worse, his pompous egoism was such that he could
bring himself to write this to the girl he hoped to marry. As his
brother says, with a wit that is probably not as unconscious as
it pretends to be: "The acquisition of a mistress was not to him
a simple and casual affair . . . before he could accept such an
entanglement he had to be sure that a mistress could be made
part of the organized pattern of his life."[12]

His ponderousness here is not linked with any real seriousness
of intent. It is connected rather to his vanity. He wanted to
know how the affair would appear, how it would affect his
position in the eyes of those he wished to impress. His brother
believes, though there seems to be no direct evidence, that he
was morbidly fearful of being known to be half-Jewish. (How
odd, and yet how characteristic, that the examples of Disraeli
and Rothschild had not purged his fear that this would militate
against worldly success.) His *Who's Who* entry is amusing
because of its boastfulness. (If he had thought for a moment, he
would have remembered that really distinguished people write
very modest *Who's Who* entries.) He was ashamed of his first
name Alphonse, and entered himself in *Who's Who* as Alroy, a
name borrowed from Disraeli's work.

He was not always, it is true, the most accomplished of
worldlings. He failed to reflect that "Society" and artistic
society are not always identical or even compatible. He was no
doubt surprised when forced to resign from one of his favourite
clubs because the members would not tolerate his having Lord
Alfred Douglas as a guest.[13]

His brother's summary seems just: "My brother's life . . . has
interest because . . . it is a revelation in microcosm of the gay,
desperate, but in the last resort always vain, assault that the
adventurer makes upon society. . . . Behind the impulse to
conquest lies always, uncontrollable, the terror of defeat."
("The gambler wishes always in his heart to lose. He is only
content when he is ruined.")[14] Probably, he was one of those

who knew in his heart that the things he sought were of little worth; and one who was troubled by his inability to love. In one of his saddest and most telling phrases, his brother writes: "he demanded an unrestrained affection which he was unable to return."[15]

His understanding of literature was, in the main, superficial. We have already seen how he misrepresented the great tradition of Victorian biography. Misled by Poe (one of his greatest heroes), he believed that "*Paradise Lost*, like all epics, loses by its length, and is read, in effect, even by its admirers, as a collection of short poems."[16] In short, he had most of the prejudices and limitations that might be expected of a man of rather uncritical mind, who had been steeped in a bad critical tradition, and had been inclined to take Oscar Wilde's paradoxes more seriously than they were meant.

But—and this remains surprising, in its contrast to the evidence given in the last paragraph—he was by no means devoid of tact and good judgment. An example is his use of the comparatively new influence of academic psychology. He makes a decisive break with Lytton Strachey by using his reading of Freud and Adler and by speaking openly of Rolfe's sexual constitution and experience; and he attributes his numerous quarrels to paranoia. There is no trace of the fault one might expect to find in a man so conscious of fashion, and so vague in his general intellectual bearings. He does not present the new theories as a philosopher's stone. His use of them is both discreet and balanced; and his treatment of the darker side of Rolfe's life is free from all scandal-mongering and sensationalism. He convinces us that his aim is simply to discover and tell what Rolfe was really like. Fears of triviality are aroused in us when he writes: "A biographer should choose his subject as a dandy chooses his suit. . . . His subjects should fit his talent as the suit fits the dandy's body: exquisitely."[17] But the fears prove to be largely groundless.

Yet for all his seriousness, we must be aware of a certain naiveté. Thus, he has obviously not really considered the problems involved in fictional self-portraiture when he writes of Rolfe's *Hadrian VII*: "this man starts to instant life in Fr. Rolfe's pages, for the best of all reasons (as I discovered later): because he was Fr. Rolfe himself."[18]

He did not, apparently, reflect that most bad novels centre

on projections of the author's desires; or how very different and difficult a thing is accurate self-portraiture. He appears to be writing on the easy (and false) assumption that we 'all see ourselves clearly in a kind of interior theatre; and this is doubly odd, because later in his book he is skilful in showing how little Rolfe really knew himself, how utterly different was the judgment of any impartial observer from his own. And the final assessment of Hadrian ("he is a superman in whom we are compelled to believe") seems very wide of the mark.[19]

Sometimes, though, we have to be on our guard against rejecting Symons' judgment too soon. Thus he quotes, without immediate comment, John Holden's account of Rolfe's search for prostitutes in Rhyl or Manchester.[20] But the reason he does not comment is not that he does not see a difficulty. The form he has chosen, one of gradual search and discovery, makes him delay his comment until much more evidence has been accumulated, and the book is nearing its end. Then he comments, sensibly enough: "Were those adventures at Rhyl true, or were they make-believe as a further disguise for his real temperament? If Rolfe did seek out those women of the street there, it was a desperate effort on his part to combat his abnormal feelings, and it failed."[21] He was less perceptive about Catholicism, and about Rolfe's persistent desire to be a priest. He writes:

> His becoming a Catholic I could easily understand. The attraction of the Catholic Faith for the artistic temperament . . . is one of the facts of psychology. Even among Rolfe's immediate contemporaries, Francis Thompson, Aubrey Beardsley, Ernest Dowson, and Lionel Johnson had followed the same path, a path which has been charted by Joris Karl Huysmans. Rolfe had become a Catholic at twenty-six; and shortly afterwards, aspired to priesthood. . . . Perhaps it is not surprising that one in whom nature had not implanted a love for women should embrace a celibate career.[22]

I postpone a general discussion of Rolfe's religion; and I hope to show that Rolfe is in important respects very different from the "ninetyish" group to whom Symons here attempts to assimilate him, while the treatment of the complex issue of Rolfe's wish to be a priest is superficial. This should not surprise us much. Religion was the point where Rolfe and Symons were furthest apart; and the latter does not seem to have made any vigorous attempt to understand it. It is surprising, though, that he does not appear to dissent from the clear misjudgment of Vincent O'Sullivan: "if the Catholics had kept him as priest he would have done them credit and might have been useful."[23] (It is a common misconception, which O'Sullivan's "kept" might seem to endorse, that Rolfe actually was ordained. Symons, of course, knows better.) Even if priesthood had helped Rolfe to restrain his homosexual tendencies, his pride and egoism would have made him a disastrously bad priest.

Symons' investigations brought him both reliable and unreliable sources, and judgments both perceptive and obtuse. I have not been able to decide with certainty why he gives us so little indication of their relative value. Was it that he did not know the difference, or that he wished to allow the reader the privilege of deciding for himself? In any event, he presents a bad source like O'Sullivan in much the same way as an extremely good one, like Canon Carmont.

Carmont is right on the mark when he says: "There was a sort of ruthless selfishness in him which led him to exploit others, quite regardless of their interest or feelings or advantage. . . . He was dressy and particular about his appearance. Church matters were mostly a matter of millinery to him."[24] And again: "Take him all in all, he was not very human: he was a sort of sub-species. He must have been very tough and elastic, or he would have been utterly crushed by the opposition and enmity he met with, and did so much to excite. Was there an element of greatness in him to account for this? Or was it perhaps something more analogous to that appalling saying of Parolles: 'If my heart were great 'twould burst at this. . . . Simply the thing I am shall make me live'?".[25]

On Rolfe's unreliability, vindictiveness and proneness to lying, Symons' sources all told him much the same story, and led him right. A particularly interesting point is brought out by Holden. Rolfe partly thought of quarrelling as an art. He was on one occasion delighted to receive an insulting letter because he enjoyed its style.[26] And a surprising reconciliation was the result. Similarly, his "undying" enmity might alternate rapidly with friendliness and approval.[27]

Symons quotes, but does not really use in his interpretation, a most interesting letter of Rolfe's to Mrs. Pirie-Gordon, which shows that he had a partial understanding of his own tendency to ingratitude:

> You all watch my words for indications of my tastes and wants in order that you may gratify them. . . . And I can do nothing adequate in return. That makes these favours hard to bear. But what makes it harder still is the knowledge that you dear kind souls, *who have given me so long the hospitality which not a single Catholic would dream of giving*, are adding to my burdens. . . . Do not give me luxuries at all which it will hurt me to lose, and help me to live so that I have nothing which can be taken from me.[28]

Symons has a sound understanding of Rolfe's paranoia, and what Osbert Sitwell called "the particular rabid bite, by the scar of which it was always possible to recognize those who had fed him."[29] He writes:

> When the film came over the eyes of his mind, Rolfe saw himself as a permanently picturesque figure oppressed by a circle of jealous enemies of his talents or exhibiting their own meanness. It was his compensation for the maddening sense of his failure, for his poverty, for his inability to dominate circumstances as he desired. Not, however, always. For those who stop on the hither side of insanity, there must be moments of self-realization, moments when an interior mentor whispers "I am wrong; they are right."[30]

We may accept this, subject to two caveats. Symons has a tendency to belittle the exercise of the will, and consequently the moral element in Rolfe's enmities. Proclaiming that all lives have a "pattern,"[31] he undervalues the unexpected, the gratuitous, the element of pure freedom, of which the life of Rolfe, like all others, provides conspicuous examples. Why, for instance, did this man who normally rewarded his benefactors with Sitwell's "rabid bite" never quarrel with his Oxford friend, E. G. Hardy, one of the kindest and most persistent of them? We may say, and this applies in varying degrees to other facets of Rolfe's life and personality, that Symons did not distinguish clearly enough between the two senses of mystery. The form of his book (properly enough) tends to assimilate his quest to a detective's search for truth in a "mystery thriller." But his duty as a biographer was also to respect that inviolable mystery of personality before which the most penetrating analysis must finally fall silent. At times, Symons' somewhat over-confident analysis of Rolfe contrasts a little oddly with his reluctance to comment on his own informants. Thus he prints five pages of varied material from Trevor Hadden without comment.[32] This is part of the uncritical attitude to sources noted earlier.

One of the most interesting and complex letters unearthed by Symons' investigation was that to Temple Scott. Here Rolfe, possibly at his most sincere and least mannered, outlines his attitude to friendship, love and passion:

> I am struck aghast every now and then by the strange thing people call Love. One would be silly to deny it— because every now and then an example crops up of a sensible man or woman having their life tangled up with the life of another in blind mystery. They actually support each the continual presence of the other. Oh, there must be something in it.
>
> But it seems so excessively funny to me. Carnal pleasure I thoroughly appreciate, but I like a change sometimes. Even partridges get tiresome after many days. Only besotted ignorance or hypocrisy demurs to carnal lust, but I meet people who call that holy which is purely natural. . . .
>
> Some talk of wickedness, and vulgarly confound the general with the particular. Of course you're wicked, every instant that you spend uncontemplative of, uncorresponding to, the Grace and Glory of your maker. That may be forgiven, for that Real Love forgives. . . .
>
> As for me, I am rotting in my chains, and Nature only looks in at my prison window, and passes by. Mail of icy indifference encloses me, no one touches me where I can feel. I am aloof—alone.[33]

On this and similar passages, Symons comments in his final summary: "He pictured impossible situations in which ambiguous figures thawed that mail of icy reserve which 'only one dead heart has ever been warm enough to melt'. . . . His forbidden love was a source of weakness, but hate could make him strong."[34]

Symons is slightly elliptical here. But he did, I think, grasp the vital connection between Rolfe's homosexual indulgence (never associated in the slightest degree with affection), his longing for a single, supreme and pure friendship of equals, his constant disappointment in failing to achieve or even approach this, and his violent gestures of enmity towards those who, through no fault of their own, proved not to be the single, divinely-given friend.

But Symons, perhaps because of his original determination to see Rolfe too much in terms of the group of writers of the 1890s, from whom he differed so much, does not stress, as he might have done, the absolute gulf there was for Rolfe between homosexual conduct and this divine friendship. There is no question, as there was for Wilde and others, of a merging of the two. When Rolfe writes of homosexuality, he invariably does so in the coarsest, most brutal way. He can only write of it when all his higher aspirations, whether toward God or the imaginary friend, are laid asleep. His higher and lower nature can never be on stage together. There is absolutely nothing corresponding to the wistful talk about the love that dare not speak its name. And the imagined, long-desired, impossible perfect friendship is utterly chaste.

Robert Hugh Benson was perhaps the friend of whom Rolfe had the strongest hopes. Symons attempts a comparison between the two men, which is unconvincing, since they were utterly different in their temperament and moral nature, and alike only in the obvious respect that both were Catholic converts. But Symons does show a virtue which many biographers lack; he does not see everything from the point of view of his own subject. He enters into Benson's disappointment and exasperation, and gives him credit for his extraordinary patience and good humour in the face of insult and slander. Here Rolfe's malice reached a new depth of childishness, when he threatened to have an obscene book published as the work of Benson. The fact that Benson was a priest, and one who might be supposed to have the ear of archbishops and cardinals, was important to Rolfe in a way Benson, thinking mainly of literary collaboration, may not have realized. Benson had died in 1914, the year after Rolfe, and long before the beginning of Symons' quest. So his favourite method of questioning his witnesses has to change. We sense that he is a little uneasy at reverting to the use of dead documents, the ordinary tools of the biographer. But his summary is fair:

> The friendship with Benson was of a deeper order than the rest. The lonely Rolfe had been sought out, had been praised, had been admitted as his superior, by one who had won the coveted, delusory haven of holy orders, and might be the means of bringing the never relinquished panacea within reach of the thirsty sufferer. So at first he felt. Afterwards, as Benson recovered his natural dominance, Rolfe's warmth diminished; and when he was, as he felt, "betrayed," shut off from even literary association . . . his liking turned to rage.[35]

Though Symons was not well-informed about Catholicism, the book is entirely free from anti-Catholic prejudice. I take it that "delusory" does not mean that the Catholic sacramental doctrine is a delusion, but rather, that Rolfe, being the man he was, could not have found a haven of peace by the simple fact of being ordained. With this, one can certainly agree.

In general Symons seems to let Rolfe off rather lightly, except on one important point, his attempts to corrupt Venetian boys by bribes for homosexual purposes:

> His ingratitude to those who helped him, his objurations against his friends, even his vindictive attempts to secure such revenge as lay in his power against those who, in his fancy, had injured him, can be explained and almost excused. He had some ground for a grudge against the world in which he found himself so misplaced, which offered such slight reward for his gifts, and the books in which they were manifested. There was some ground for his grudge against Benson. But if these dark letters are to be believed, he had embarked in Venice on a course of life which not even well-founded wrongs, even by his own standard could justify. . . . He had become a habitual corrupter of youth, a seducer of innocence. . . . Neither scruple nor remorse was expressed or implied in these long accounts of his sexual exploits and enjoyments.[36]

Some, notably Donald Weeks,[37] have taken the view that

Rolfe's homosexual letters are merely fantasies. But it seems to me clear that Symons is in the right on this.

We may note with amusement the intrusion of Symons' own personality and money troubles in his quaint statement of the belief that the world owes the artist a living (however extravagant he may be); and we may disagree with the view that Rolfe had any reason for serious complaint against Benson. But we can hardly dissent from the condemnation.

If we step back and look at Symons' book as a whole, the verdict may be that he is very good at discovering things, very open-minded in accepting evidence that seems to point in different directions, but that in the end he just fails to focus his subject. Probably this is due at the same time to his method and his personality. The influence of the first here will be obvious; of his personality we may say that he was blind and deaf to the spiritual. Rolfe's degradation was a spiritual one. Something of what is missing is supplied in Graham Greene's essay: "For if ever there was a case of demoniac possession it was Rolfe's: the hopeless piety, the screams of malevolence, the sense of despair which to a man of his faith was the sin against the Holy Ghost. . . . The greatest saints have been men with more than normal capacity for evil, and the most vicious men have sometimes narrowly evaded sanctity."[38]

And of Symons' informants, Greene writes: "they cannot understand the eccentricity of a man who chooses to go about sheathed in flame in the heyday of the Entente Cordiale, of Sir Ernest Cassel and Lily Langtry."[39] Greene also observes: "The many excellent men and women, who did their best, sometimes an unimaginative best, to help Rolfe, here caper like demons. . . . It is instructive and entertaining to see the great and good for once from the devil's point of view."[40]

In Rolfe, the old adage, so often found true by students of sanctity, "The greater the sinner, the greater the saint," receives its shocking and terrible obverse. Of all this Symons is a good-humoured, fair-minded but uncomprehending witness.

III

If we feel the need, as we do, to go beyond Symons in our understanding of Rolfe, it is partly, no doubt, a tribute to the curiosity his book arouses. I have said that Rolfe seems to me very different from the group of 1890s writers to whom Symons tried to assimilate him—and much more different as a man than he is as a writer. Perhaps his leading characteristic was a complete absence of fluidity of temperament. His personality seems to stand in gigantic blocks. It is like a statue made of various hard substances, granite, iron, marble, which can never be fused, and which gives an impression of the monstrous because of the unprecedented strangeness of their being brought together in the portrayal of a single body. Rolfe never wavers (as for instance, Oscar Wilde does) between Christianity and aestheticism, or between the love of women and the love of men. (It is a pity Symons never finished his life of Wilde, of which interesting fragments remain.[41]) Rolfe never wavers, though he sometimes oscillates with inconceivable violence and rapidity, from one extreme to another.

As we would expect, religion and sex reveal most clearly his unlikeness to the 1890s model. His Catholicism was schematic and uncompromising; his faith, for all that it had so little influence on conduct, seems to have been very strong. Rebellion and despair, not doubt, were its negative side. And it was a very ecclesiastical faith; not only in superficial ways, such as love of ceremony, but in a stubborn insistence that the Roman Church was exactly what it claimed to be. Two examples of this will suffice. He was habitually scornful of the Anglican Church for its Erastianism; and he rejected the offer of a schismatic bishopric in a small, ancient Indian community, the Syro-Chaldean.[42] The decisiveness with which he did so is at first sight surprising. The offer could have seemed like the solution of all his difficulties, the end of all his humiliations, at a stroke. He had longed to be a priest, had been rejected, and now he might become not a priest but a bishop. The gorgeous robes on which his imagination dwelt would have been provided; and his financial position would at least have been improved. Above all, he would have taken a spectacular revenge on those who had (so wisely) prevented his ordination as a Catholic. But the only questions he asked about it were Catholic questions. "Are the orders valid?" and "are they in communion with Rome?" Unless both questions could be answered in the affirmative, he would not consider it. As usual, he did not waver.

So much about his religion is clear. But there are obscurities. What are we to make of his vow of celibacy? On January 5, 1910, in his fiftieth year, he wrote to Monsignor (later Cardinal) Bourne, Archbishop of Westminster:

> I beg leave again to remind your Grace that I am an ecclesiastic subject of your archdiocese, expelled from the Scots College of Rome in 1890 as having no Vocation, but still a Tonsured Clerk & persisting in my Divine Vocation to the priesthood. I should say also, that my vow of twenty years' celibacy (which I offered in proof of my Vocation) expires this year, & that I am not at all moved to avail myself of liberty, but propose to renew my vow for life at the year's end.[43]

Against this we must set, not only his homosexuality, but his engrained aversion to women, recorded by Holden in his letter to Symons:

> The worst of a woman is that she expects you to make love to her, or to pretend to make love to her, first.
> What you can see to admire in the female form I don't know. All those curves and protuberances that seem to fascinate you only go to show what nature intended her for—all that she's fit for—breeding.[44]

And much more in the same vein.

Was his letter to Monsignor Bourne the grossest hypocrisy? And on the subject (priesthood) which of all others was sacred to him? Did he inwardly mean that he had been abstinent in denying satisfaction to his own different sexual urges? (But it seems most unlikely that he had been so abstinent. So the hypocrisy would be no less.) Did his perverse mind see celibacy, not as a sacrifice of the blessing of marriage, but as a rejection of woman and the flesh as evil? Was he so deep a liar that he did not know he lied? Or was he having a private joke with himself under the guise of a solemn protest?

Then a question Symons evaded is bound to force itself upon anyone who thinks about Rolfe. What was the relation, for him, of faith and sin? The phrases which may seem fairly appropriate to many 1890s Catholics, phrases like "weakness of the flesh," miss the mark when applied to Rolfe. He hardly seems to be aware of sin except in other people. Was he antinomian? It would be strange indeed if this staunch Catholic exemplified this ultra-Protestant heresy. But strangeness is so much the mark of everything about Rolfe, that we cannot immediately rule out the possibility. Was he tortured by guilt, but too proud ever to admit it? There is often a strong strain of self-righteousness in his quarrels, and he may honestly have believed he was not much to blame there; he may have been unaware of his own egoism. But it would surely have been harder for him to justify to himself his lying and his sexual conduct.

But in all this, we must be careful not to expect full sanity of a man who was so unbalanced, and remember the truth expressed by D. H. Lawrence: "It is all amazing, that a man with so much insight and fineness . . . should be so helpless and just purely ridiculous, when it comes to actualities."[45]

Lawrence also said (of *Hadrian the Seventh*) "it does not 'date' as do Huysmans' books, or Wilde's or the rest of them. Only a first-rate book escapes its date."[46] In my own view, Lawrence here praises the book too highly. But whether we agree or not, there is no doubt that Lawrence was right in pointing to Rolfe's uniqueness, his refusal to be categorized, which makes speculation particularly hazardous. To ask, for instance, what his confessions may have been like, is to move at once into the realm not only of the unknown but of the entirely unimaginable.

Tentatively, and without any assurance of being right, I would suggest that his condition in his later years arose from an amalgam of two separate and partly opposite impulses: theological despair, and a desire, by piling sin on sin, to punish God for not taking him at his own valuation and making him a priest. Certainly his tendency to blame all the crimes, failures and misfortunes of his life on the fact that he was not a priest is well-documented. We rightly treat this as special pleading; we know that priesthood would not have saved him. All the same, his obsession with the subject may be the pointer to the deepest inward truth. If what I suggest is accepted, it would be consistent with, and partly help to explain two puzzling features of the case. One has already been mentioned: his apparent absence of guilt in performing acts (sexual and other) which the ordinary teaching of the Church holds to be sinful. The other feature is his persistent, loudly-proclaimed hatred of his fellow-

Catholics. For instance, in a letter to the secretary of the Fabian Society of February 15, 1906 he wrote: "Mr. Rolfe encloses a subscription of Five Shillings. He is not a Socialist. ... He is a Roman Catholic; & finds the Faith comfortable & the faithful intolerable: consequently he is not even on speaking terms with Roman Catholics."[47]

This goes far beyond ordinary quarrelsomeness. Even in writing to someone he did not know, and cannot have supposed to be a Catholic or to have Catholic sympathies, we find the inexorable wish to separate himself from other Catholics. If he was trying to punish them, the effort was a feeble one. But there would be a crazy consistency if he were inwardly blaming God.

At least, that mood of rebellion and blame would be the normal one. But there were moments of intermission, when a tender pleading took its place. The most poignant example, perhaps, is the poem of January 1910 (the same month as his letter to Monsignor Bourne quoted above), sent to the *Tablet*, but rejected. Under the Greek word $'IX\Phi Y\Sigma$ (fish), an ancient acronym for Jesus Christ, Son of God and Saviour, he wrote:

"Or, if he ask a fish," (he—the son) "will he give him a serpent?"
Yea: to the least of Thy sons, that is just what they give.
Christ, in response to Thy Call, I ardently asked to be number'd, lustrums five ago, on the roll of Thy priests:
proof of that Call there is none, save this—my unfailing assertion vowing a bare bed, still persevering alone.
Also, I asked for the love of a friend which beareth, believeth, hopeth, endureth, all things, nor ever shall fail. . . .
King, I appeal from this gang of tormentors, malignant or stupid:
not unto man any more do I cry, but to Thee—[48]

Such, not undignified, were his lucid moments. But if his anger against God had occasional intermissions, his anger against men had fewer and fewer. We may say, if we like, that he was a paranoiac, but remember at the same time that his anger against men was also felt, perhaps, as a way of punishing God.

His rigid and exclusive homosexuality, and his detestation of women, mark him off yet again from many nineties writers. Wilde,

John Addington Symonds and others were sufficiently bisexual to marry and father children. Their homosexual adventures could be seen either as yielding to temptation or as maintaining a deliberate kind of artistic pose. Either way, they were entirely different from Rolfe, for whom heterosexual love appeared as abnormality and perversity. We can relate this difference not only to difference of sexual constitution and desire, but also (perhaps more importantly) to a deep difference in attitudes to the world. The others wished to please the world; and took its heterosexuality, as most people do, as part of what is unarguably given, one of the conditions of life, almost like time and space. But Rolfe at the deepest level cared nothing for the world. His terrifying solitariness is more than a social fact; it penetrated to the depths of his spirit. He was his own norm and standard. He was able by a monstrous act of pride to "excommunicate" all women and all normal men. We are very far from the world of the 1890s here.

We must not, however, because of the extreme intensity of his deeper nature, fall into the temptation of presenting him as more absolute, more all of one piece, than the evidence shows him to have been. How surprising, for instance, that he could be a delightful tutor who wrote playful, and much-enjoyed letters like this:

My dear John,

I am sorry to hear that you have gotten the measles. The question is How many measles have you gotten? For my part I think one ought not to be greedy about them, like the boy who took all that there were in the neighbourhood & so covered himself with pimples that he was quite unable to see out of his eyes for nearly a fortnight. That, of course, was very annoying for him: but consider how disgusted all the other boys of that place must have been when they found there was not a single measle left for them to share between them. . . . I suppose you know what an extraordinary city this is where I am living. Ask Mother or Father to tell you about it. I send you a map so that you can see for yourself how it is built on little islands in the sea, so that we have to go about in boats. . . . Not a sound to be heard, but footsteps in the great Square of Saint Mark where I live.[49]

This letter is dated February 27, 1909, less than a year before the anguished poem and the letter to Monsignor Bourne.

The surface details of his life were just as full of contrasts as the depths. Take these two contrasting pictures, the first by Rolfe himself, the second by an observer:

> The last few days I have been anchored near an empty island, Sacca Fisola, not too far away from civilization to be out of reach of fresh water, but lonely enough for dying alone in the boat if need be. . . . If I stay out on the lagoon, the boat will sink, I shall swim perhaps for a few hours, and then I shall be eaten alive by crabs. At low water every mudbank swarms with them. If I stay anchored near an island, I must keep continually awake: for the moment I cease moving, I am invaded by swarms of swimming rats, who in the winter are so voracious that they attack every man who is motionless. I have tried it. And have been bitten. Oh my dear man you can't think how artful fearless ferocious they are. . . . They bit my toes and woke me shrieking and shaking with fear.[50]

And J. C. Powys wrote this about Rolfe:

> Somewhere down by the Rialto, in a very crowded and very narrow canal, we encountered . . . a floating equipage that resembled the barge of Cleopatra, or perhaps I ought rather to say that ship, so often delineated in Greek vase paintings, that carried the great god Dionysus on his triumphant voyage. This other gondola, whose high ornamental poop collided with our own, was actually covered with the most wonderful skins of leopards and lynxes and it was handled by a Being who might very well have passed for the Faun of Praxiteles. In the stern, lying on a leopard's skin, was a personage who, as I learnt later, was one of the most whimsical writers and one of the most beguiling men of the great world.[51]

Perhaps it does not matter whether we fully believe the first account, for in any case it describes one part of his inner, imaginative world as eloquently as Powys describes the other. Perhaps no one has ever lived so little as Rolfe did in the ordinary middle world that is the world of all of us.

Finally, how to sum up our verdict on Symons? His success was in finding information; his failure was a failure of knowledge. He did not know enough about the Catholic Church, about the Victorian age, about literature, about biography. Thus he was often unable to put his fascinating material in context, or to evaluate it accurately. He discovered a lot, but he did not know enough.

CHAPTER FIVE

Richard Ellmann's
James Joyce

PHILLIP F. HERRING

Many biographical subjects would applaud Miss Bordereau's condemnation of her inquisitive adversary in Henry James' *The Aspern Papers* as a "publishing scoundrel,"[1] or even assent to Joyce's word—"biografiend."[2] Few would contest Germaine Greer's point that today the general reader prefers Boswell to Johnson, so that a biographer's exploitation extends beyond subject to readership as well. Greer's description of literary biography as "a progressive disease" is excessive, as is her statement that "Giving your body to medical research is one thing; throwing your mind to the jackals is another," but she does rightly point to the normally—even properly—adversarial relationship of biographer to famous personage.[3] Few people wish to "tell all," preferring instead to censor in advance by destroying letters or drafts, or to hide unpleasant truths by devious means. Surviving friends and relatives normally know and respect their wish for privacy. Biographers, on the other hand, align themselves with journalists on questions of censorship, free speech and the public's right to know, but they sometimes lack taste.

Although censorship caused James Joyce frequent grief early in his career as a writer, he was not loath to censor others when the image he wished to project stood in jeopardy. Herbert Gorman discovered this to his cost at the end of 1930, some eleven years before Joyce's demise, when he was invited to write an "authorized" biography of the Irish writer.[4] This meant that he was allowed to gather factual evidence from reluctant people for what could only be described as a hagiography. As Richard Ellmann says, Joyce "made clear that he was to be treated as a saint with an unusually protracted martyrdom" (*JJ2*, 631).[5] Joyce's all-too-human desire to control Gorman resulted in a biography reliable in most instances, but factually, critically and intellectually anemic, one which should be consulted today only as a curiosity.

In writing the second biography of Joyce, Richard Ellmann had some important advantages over Gorman: one biography, however inadequate, had already appeared. Joyce was already dead and could not interfere. Most candidates for interview were still alive, and were inclined to lay aside loyalty and reticence to tell what they knew. In his narrative skills and in the thoroughness of his research, many would argue that Ellmann is one of the two or three most gifted literary biographers of the twentieth century—perhaps the best. Since no future biographer will have access to more than a handful of people who knew Joyce, a serious rival to Ellmann's biography is scarcely conceivable.

ELLMANN'S THEORY OF BIOGRAPHY

Something of Ellmann's philosophy of biography may be gleaned from *James Joyce* itself, but systematic expositions are to be found in his chapter "Literary Biography" in *Golden Codgers* (1973) and in "Freud and Literary Biography" (1984). These essays offer critiques of major biographies, especially those indebted to Freudian techniques or concepts, and define Ellmann's own common sense position with respect to Freudian theory, a position considerably less venturesome than, for example, Leon Edel's. He acknowledges that any modern biographer must be indebted to Freud: "The biographer conceives of himself not as outside but as inside the subject's mind, not as observing but as ferreting."[6]

Ellmann also expresses opinions on other modern biographers. For instance, he grants Jean-Paul Sartre's biography of Flaubert a certain fascination and power, while expressing amazement at the confidence with which Sartre fabricates a life by reading the fiction.[7] Earlier he had juxtaposed Sartre's theory of biography to that of Erik Erikson, the author of *Young Man Luther*: "Sartre says, if it didn't happen this way, it happened in some way like it; Erikson says, if it didn't happen, it as good as happened.

But he seems, in comparison with Sartre, cavalier in not admitting when he is being speculative, when historical."[8] We shall consider later how well Ellmann manages to avoid these pitfalls himself.

Ellmann requires that modern biographers be allowed what I call "biographical license" in portraiture. Speculation, even in the absence of factual support, he deems indispensable: "Biographies will continue to be archival, but the best ones will offer speculations, conjectures, hypotheses."[9] He says further, "Today we want to see our great men at their worst as well as their best; we ask of biographers the same candour that our novelists have taught us to accept from them."[10]

THE FIRST EDITION OF *JAMES JOYCE* (1959)

This work is an 842-page chronological narrative of immense detail, divided into five sections: Part I explores the Dublin years, showing the descent into poverty of Joyce's family, occasioned by his father's drinking and improvidence. Young James is increasingly alienated from home, Church and country, eventually undergoing transformation from conscientious Catholic pupil into radical thinker. In 1904 at the age of twenty-two he elopes to the Continent with a chambermaid from Galway, Nora Barnacle. Ellmann includes considerable detail on the biographical background to *A Portrait of the Artist as a Young Man, Ulysses* and, to some extent, *Dubliners*. In 1907 a slim volume of poems is published—*Chamber Music*.

Part II chronicles the years of poverty in Pola and Trieste, where Joyce taught English at the Berlitz school, and in Rome, where he worked in a bank. Two children are born, Giorgio and Lucia. Ellmann discusses the backgrounds to *Ulysses* and the most celebrated *Dubliners* story, "The Dead." In these ten years Joyce hones his skills as a writer and, after the most difficult negotiations with publishers, sees *Dubliners* appear in book form (1914).

Part III deals with the five Zurich years (1915–20), Joyce's growing literary reputation, the publication of *A Portrait* (1916) and the writing of *Ulysses*. Part IV is about the Paris years, the publication of *Ulysses* (1922), the writing and publication of *Finnegans Wake* (1939) and the mental illness of Lucia. These are the years of Joyce the celebrity. The final part, one chapter only, recounts the family's return to Zurich from German-occupied France, and Joyce's death in 1941 from a perforated ulcer. This very bare outline of Joyce's life omits the publication of more minor works and many other important details.

Joyce once described himself to his brother Stanislaus as the foolish author of a wise book (*JJ2*, 471), and to Carl Jung as "a man of small virtue, inclined to extravagance and alcoholism."[11] Ellmann's biography provides such abundant evidence of Joyce's correct assessment of his own character on these two occasions that the reader searches in vain for evidence that, except very rarely, Joyce acted charitably towards anyone. He placed his own interests first, and exploited relatives as ruthlessly as friends. Inexplicable adversity he often attributed to Judases around him. Joyce seems to have been hopelessly impractical, gleefully self-serving and much given to biting the hands that fed him. He would have agreed with this assessment, and yet rightly believed that his genius would ultimately be triumphant over petty adversity; if there is a single theme in Ellmann's biography, this may be it.

After borrowing money and clothes from everybody he knew, Joyce eloped to the continent with a naive young Catholic woman from Galway on the flimsy evidence of a mail-order firm's testimony of a job opening in Zurich's Berlitz school. None was available. After finally landing this teaching position in Trieste, he persuaded his naive, reliable, admiring, exploitable young brother Stanislaus to move to Trieste, quickly saddling him with his own family responsibilities. While Nora had babies in the pauper ward and sniffled about the flat, and Stannie labored with nine fingers in the dyke, James frequently drank himself into an alcoholic stupor. In controlled circumstances the two salaries would have been scarcely enough; to fill the bottomless crevice of Joyce's imagined need, six or seven salaries would have been consumed as quickly.

Chapter Thirteen of Ellmann's biography treats the years 1905–1906, when Stanislaus first arrived in Trieste to seek misfortune, as, in a different way, his brother had done before him. The appropriate caption from *Finnegans Wake* reads "Enchainted, dear sweet Stainusless, young confessor, dearer dearest, we herehear, aboutobloss, O coelicola, thee salutamt" (*FW*, 237), reminding us that fraternal antagonism is an important theme and structuring device of Joyce's last work. The opening lines capture the essence of Joyce's brother:

> Stanislaus Joyce, invoked like a recalcitrant spirit by his brother, arrived in Trieste after several days of travel across the continent. The journey, marked by seasickness on the Channel and monastic economies on third- and fourth-class trains through Germany and Austria, had not been agreeable. Rightly anticipating that the larder in Trieste would be bare, Stanislaus allowed himself only two dinners, two coffees, two eggs, and a beer en route. . . . He was twenty but acted forty-five. His sober mien and his firm, broad-shouldered body gave him an air of substance that his taller, angular brother lacked. (*JJ2*, 212)

Note the exact catalogue of expenditures, which Stanislaus remembered for fifty years, long enough to tell Richard Ellmann.

What follows has about it an air of inevitability. Joyce informs his brother that he and Nora are destitute and wonders if there is money left from the trip. Stannie takes the job at the Berlitz School and agrees to fork over his salary for household expenses. "Eventually, to simplify matters, Joyce began to sign the paybook for Stanislaus and to take the money directly" (*JJ2*, 213). Exploitation continues and hostility grows, as the drunken Joyce returns home nights to be scolded and even, at times, to endure beatings by his brother. Increasingly Joyce answers Stannie's exhortations with prolonged silence.

While Ellmann has sometimes been charged with stacking the deck against Joyce by emphasizing Stanislaus' viewpoint as stated in interviews and in his book *My Brother's Keeper* (1958), the narrative of Chapter Thirteen draws on a diversity of other sources as well: letters, postcards and an interview with Alessandro Francini Bruni, Joyce's colleague and friend from the school. In one letter of December 4, 1905 to his Aunt Josephine, Joyce, apparently worried about Stannie's missives to this aunt, defends himself with typically determined self-indulgence, an important element in Ellmann's portrait of Joyce:

> I daresay I am a difficult person for any woman to put up with but on the other hand I have no intention of changing.

... I am not a very domestic animal—after all, I suppose I am an artist—and sometimes when I think of the free and happy life which I have (or had) every talent to live I am in a fit of despair. (*JJ2*, 214)

Joyce's plaintive epistles to female benefactors and confessors would in themselves make for an interesting volume of letters. There was his mother, to whom as a student in Paris he sent wheedling letters asking for money, Aunt Josephine, who filled the role after his mother's death, and later Harriet Weaver and Sylvia Beach.

Meanwhile, despite adversity, the months in Trieste passed merrily enough. Joyce entertained his students with comical exercises in English, a selection of which are quoted. Ellmann also sees in them relevant topical patterns: "Joyce's central preoccupations: his financial need, his family, his country, his irreligion, his love of literature. Wives make cuckolds; Italy is, except for the church, a fraud, and the church is an old whore; Ireland is horrible but unforgettable" (*JJ2*, 218).

Ellmann also describes Joyce's struggles to have *Chamber Music* and *Dubliners* published, and provides a useful selection of Joyce's correspondence with the publisher Grant Richards. These letters reveal that though Joyce invited adversity, he received more than his just deserts at the hands of publishers. They dawdled and demanded excisions, while Joyce, for his part, refused to understand that printers and publishers could be sent to prison for violating the laws of decency.

Chapter Thirteen has a fine symmetry about it: it begins with an arrival and ends with a departure, as Joyce, Nora and little Giorgio journey to Rome, where a position as bank clerk awaited the struggling Irish writer. Here Ellmann's fine sense of closure becomes a prelude to further adventures:

With a feeling of relief, and a conviction that Rome would yield him money and fame as it had previously done for Attila and other less civilized invaders, Joyce and Nora packed up their few belongings and, with the unbaptized Giorgio in arms, started for the Eternal City. (*JJ2*, 223)

Inevitably Joyce tired of Rome and the bank, at which time, ignoring his brother's pleas, he packed his entourage onto a train, returned to Trieste, and made himself and his family once again the responsibility of Stanislaus.

EVALUATIONS

Robert Adams called *James Joyce* "the best literary biography of our time,"[12] and most readers would agree that in this century it has few rivals for excellence. More than once the book has been placed beside such enduring works as Boswell's *Life of Johnson*. Its eloquence, irreverence and narrative power appeal to general readers as well as to scholars, as all great biographies must. The impression left is of a brilliant, witty, humane biographer writing with charitable indulgence of an artist who achieved success despite many imperfections.

Scholars have found *James Joyce* indispensable, though some point to specific imperfections; few indeed have challenged the biography's veracity in the larger sense. Such citadels are easier to attack or defend than to build, but a balanced evaluation must take into account alleged and actual shortcomings, which we shall do as a way of measuring Richard Ellmann's achievement.

Few events of momentous significance emerge from the mountain of detail that is *James Joyce*, but the same is true of Joyce's literary works. In Ellmann's biography, though, the mundane becomes fascinating—even dramatic. Like Stephen and Bloom in "Ithaca," Ellmann and Joyce followed parallel courses, with Joyce transubstantiating life experience in the chalice of his imagination to produce art and Ellmann gathering from many sources that same experience and converting it into biographical narrative. In both cases the quotidian holds our interest through the writer's humor, narrative power and interesting perspectives. Although Joyce would have disapproved of any biographer he could not control, he found his ideal biographer in Ellmann.

Katherine Frank has rightly said, "In the end one must admit that the success of *James Joyce*, for all its thematic acuteness and historical breadth and soundness, derives from [the distinctive voice of Richard Ellmann]." Her appropriate example is the gentle mockery of a love letter from Joyce which concludes "'My holy love, my darling Nora. O can it be that we are now

about to enter the heaven of our life? . . .' Before entering
heaven, it was necessary first to leave purgatory. Joyce waited
impatiently for money from Trieste, but Stanislaus could not
wrest it from Artifoni" (*JJ1*, 297).[13] Or consider an example
selected by David Greene which describes Joyce (and Stephen)
as revolutionary artist: "When he rebels he hastens to let them
know of his rebellion so that he can measure their response to
it. He searches for disciples who must share his motives
vicariously. . . . He buys his own ticket for Holyhead, but
claims to have been deported. . . . Having stomped angrily out
of the house, he circled back to peer in the window" (*JJ2*,
292).[14] One sentence suggests an important transformation:
"Before Ibsen's letter Joyce was an Irishman; after it he was a
European" (*JJ2*, 75). Horace Reynolds rightly noted that this
biography "absorbs the reader like a great novel."[15]

Disagreement as to the merit of *James Joyce* seems based in
part on varying opinions about generic rules—what should a
biography be and what kind is this one? Neither question is
easily answered. Should modern biography be literally the story
of a subject's life, or does fact and unfact serve a larger truth,
often a metaphorical one, or is this a genre akin to fiction,
where, as in all art, factual detail becomes the basis of illusion?
One finds it difficult to decide among these possibilities, and
yet to say that biography should be all these things also fails to
satisfy.

If Ellmann's skill as a raconteur is the foundation of his
biography's greatness, it is hard to lay to rest the suspicion that
in the quest of good stories a price has been paid in verifiable
factual authenticity. Inevitably there have been a few charges
of distortion, of dubious credulity in the interest of telling a
good story, or assertions that the portrait drawn of Joyce is
finally too bleak and depressing, or that Ellmann's frequent
ironical perspectives derive from too great a reliance on the
memoirs of Joyce's very strait-laced brother Stanislaus, who,
like James Duffy of "A Painful Case," was unforgiving of
behavior suggesting degeneracy.

Some reviewers have caught errors, hardly surprising in a
book of this magnitude. Kristian Smidt saw one in the dating of
a photograph subsequently omitted (*JJ1*, 272),[16] and Kenner
noted that Joyce's birthplace (not Rathmines but Rathgar) and
place of baptism were corrected in the revised edition.[17] J. B.

Bamborough notes that Ibsen did not desert his wife (*JJ1*, 221), and it is "rather misleading to say that Sir Sidney Lee's 'real name' was Simon Lazarus" (*JJ1*, 425), "nor was Arthur Symons guilty of 'taking hashish for several years'" (*JJ1*, 116).[18] In the revised edition, the points about Lee and Symons are more correctly stated. Christopher Ricks caught an error where Ellmann attributes a reference in a letter by Joyce to Emerson's essay on "Nature" which has a more precisely matching biblical source in Luke 17:20 (*JJ2*, 115n).[19] Coílín Owens and others have also found errata.

Chester Anderson caught a mistake which helps support a good story about the background of *A Portrait*, where Ellmann fabricates a non-existent row of houses on a seaside street "occasionally flooded with seawater" (*JJ1*, 23). Eileen Vance supposedly lived there, a childhood friend of Joyce whose name appears on the second page of *A Portrait*. We read that the angry Christmas dinner scene of this novel actually occurred and was overheard by the Vances "across the street" (*JJ1*, 33/34). There was no "across the street" because Martello Terrace in Bray, where these events take place, faces the sea. Anderson claims that the Vances lived in the same building as the Joyces, but the drama is enhanced by suggesting that the commotion was loud enough to be heard across the street. Anderson concludes that Ellmann seems more interested in daring, bold surmises than in details of fact.[20] But, despite the suspicion of tampering, the biographer was probably misled by the fictional context.

Joseph Prescott found more instances of Ellmann's relying on fiction for biographical evidence, "several times, without external support, [assigning] to historical persons what Joyce gave to fictional characters."[21] For example, "Ghezzi piously reminded Joyce that Bruno was a terrible heretic, and Joyce dryly rejoined, 'Yes, and he was terribly burned'" (*JJ1*, 61). Ellmann's footnote cites *A Portrait* as his source. Two pages later we read "Joyce retorted, according to *A Portrait*, 'If you must have a Jesus, let it be a legitimate Jesus'" (*JJ1*, 63). Of the Fenian Joseph Casey, we are told "Casey made his way later to Paris where, Joyce said, he was 'unsought by any save by me'" (*JJ1*, 130), the source for this comment being *Ulysses*. Hurrying home from Paris to his dying mother's side, Joyce "crossed at Newhaven and spoke broken English on the pier to avoid tipping a porter to carry his bag" (*JJ1*, 133), because Stephen remembers having done so in *Ulysses*. Joyce's father had a "low opinion of [Oliver] Gogarty, whom he called 'the counterjumper's son'" since Simon Dedalus does so in the "Hades" episode of *Ulysses*. Prescott also cites phrases such as "if the evidence of *Ulysses* can be trusted" (*JJ1*, 103); later there is the suggestion that *A Portrait* "has led some readers to suppose that Joyce could not bear his own hero" (*JJ1*, 149–150), a conjecture Ellmann does not support with evidence.

Arnold Goldman also objected to Ellmann's "often easy amalgamation of Joyce's life and fiction, especially *A Portrait of the Artist as a Young Man*, or incorporation of fiction into biography":

> As has been pointed out, there are occasions when no other source for the imputed event exists other than the novel. Professor Ellmann has not been able to resist inserting into his new text W. P. D'Arcy's story, in a letter to him, that Alfred H. Hunter took Joyce home after a "fracas" in St. Stephen's Green. The biography then backs off, in a way unusual for Ellmann. "If Dublin report can be trusted," he writes, "Joyce was said to have been dusted off and taken home . . ." "Other confirmation is lacking," says Ellmann's note. Hunter himself has been taken out and dusted off here, for Ellmann had rather demoted his claims as a Dublin model for Bloom in 1959, in favour of Charles Chance.[22]

Ellmann's defense might be that such biographical license serves the interest of a higher truth, being deceptive only when the fictional source is undocumented.

The unwillingness to grant such license has prompted Hugh Kenner, in what is one of the harshest reviews of either edition of *James Joyce*, to coin the term "Irish Fact, definable as anything they tell you in Ireland."[23] The implication is that the Irish are always game for a leg-pull. Kenner says "Ellmann's handling obeys certain imperatives, as that no good story should be rejected,"[24] citing Ellmann's inability to resist the story about Hunter fed to him by W. P. D'Arcy, the untrustworthy source mentioned by Goldman. Ellmann hedges his story with the statement "if Dublin report can be trusted" (*JJ2*, 161), but in the afterword to the Penguin edition of *Ulysses*, he recounts the Hunter story again as if it actually happened.[25]

Kenner said that Ellmann was probably the victim of a hoax perpetrated by Brian O'Nolan, who claimed to have authored a purported interview with Joyce's father.[26] Kenner also complained that the advertised definitiveness of *James Joyce* was undercut by Ellmann's tendency to exploit promising fictional material. Kenner's conclusion is that, although by no means definitive, "this is the best [biography] we are likely to see" even if "It was skewed from the start, for one thing, by a prime source, Stanislaus Joyce."[27]

In a letter to me of September 4, 1986, Kenner summarized his position on the Ellmann biography: "(1) E. has no sense whatever of the nature of Irish anecdotal testimony; (2) that this blindness is in part willed, since skepticism of such sources would have reduced the biography's length by 1/3; (3) that between his often deficient literary sense and his desire to make a *big* book, he has attached his facts and unfacts to an imagined Joyce who stuck slavishly to 'experience' (thus everything in the books must have somehow 'happened'); and (4) that his pervasive condescension to his subject has shaped his refusal to really correct anything in 'revising.' "

Ellmann wrote me on August 5, 1986, to rebut Kenner's objections as remembered from the *TLS* review. He denied that the interview of John Joyce was a hoax and says so in a note in the revised paperback edition of the biography. He continues:

As to D'Arcy's identifications, I had a long correspondence with D'Arcy, who if he is alive is over ninety, and concluded from it that he was unreliable. There was a complicated system of crosschecking which I used, and nothing was taken for granted. As to Stanislaus' testimony, you will recall that I was the first to point out their strained relations, and I took nothing on faith. Fortunately, Joyce's letters to Stanislaus confirm or deny what Stanislaus wrote, and there was of course other testimony, such as Eileen's and Eva's, Francini Bruni's, etc.

It is still unclear why, if D'Arcy was unreliable, his story was

mentioned at all in the biography or the Penguin edition of
Ulysses.

From a decidedly Catholic perspective, William Noon, S. J.,
objected that Ellmann's easygoing attitude towards Joyce's
apostasy belied the importance which the Irish writer attached
both to his struggle with the Church and to questions of
spiritual values; Joyce preferred not "disdain to combat," as
Ellmann says, but rather the opposite. This suggested to Noon
a lifelong struggle with belief and a remorse of conscience
which Ellmann fails to take into account, resulting in a tone
which is consistently inappropriate when matters of faith are in
question. On the biography's last page (first edition), Ellmann
also neglected to recount Nora Joyce's return to the faith, her
wish for the last rites of the Church, a parish church funeral
and a Catholic burial.[28] The late Father Noon would not have
been satisfied with Ellmann's treatment of this matter in the
revised edition:

> Nora Joyce died of uremic poisoning on April 10, 1951. She
> had not renounced Catholicism as thoroughly as her husband,
> and in her last years she occasionally went to church and
> prayer. When she was dying at the convent hospital she
> allowed a priest to be brought, and received the last rites. At
> her funeral a priest delivered, after the Swiss custom, a
> funeral speech at the grave. (*JJ2*, 743)

In letters to the editor of the *James Joyce Quarterly*, Robert
Scholes rebutted Noon, suggesting that the priesthood was
hoping for a posthumous conversion for Joyce, and in the next
issue of *JJQ* Ruth von Phul took a third position rather hostile
to Scholes.[29]

Let us return for a moment to the question of Ellmann's
tone. He undoubtedly takes some liberties with his subject, but
since this is part of a lively style which makes for absorbing
reading, one hesitates to criticize tone except where it leads us
astray. Ellmann is witty, a great virtue in a biographer, and the
joy he feels in his narrative power may overflow in occasional
barbs that surprise us with their sting. Niall Montgomery, for
instance, found certain passages of the biography gratuitously
offensive in tone, among them one concerning Joyce's
schizophrenic daughter:

If Lucia's malady had been curable, Joyce's jumpy supervision would have been reprehensible; since it was incurable, his obstinate moving from doctor to doctor was at least proof of his affection. (*JJ1*, 674)

Montgomery also demonstrated that Ellmann's quips can be erroneous in implication, as when he includes Joyce's rival Oliver Gogarty in "loud-mouthed, burly" company (*JJ1*, 228);[30] on the other hand, Ellmann also said of Gogarty: "He would one day be a famous surgeon and poet; that is, he would be famous as a surgeon to his readers and as a poet to his patients" (*JJ2*, 117). For such wit, much can be forgiven, but there are limits.

JOYCE'S POLITICS

My article "Joyce's Politics," written in 1969 amid Vietnam protests, attacked Joyce for self-serving political attitudes.[31] The polemical rhetoric I attribute to my naive reliance on the Ellmann biography, to which eleven of fifteen footnotes are credited. To the unsuspecting, biographers seem amanuenses of some loftier truth, and great biographies often appear to be definitive precisely in those areas where they offer only partial views. Then, too, during a time of national crisis it is not easy to justify energy expended on a writer whose politics seem egocentric and ignoble, though all the questioning of authority current in the Sixties should have made us more suspicious of biographies as well.

Since then Dominic Manganiello's *Joyce's Politics*, Colin MacCabe's *James Joyce and the Revolution of the Word* and various feminist studies, to name only Joyce studies, have demonstrated what few of us could see in 1969—that criticism and theory can help us penetrate to levels of significance beyond what we can learn from letters alone. The evidence of the letters and the Trieste lectures contained in *The Critical Writings of James Joyce* show but a one-dimensional portrait, the stuff of biography, what Joyce said to his friends. The subject interests us, after all, not so much for what subtle, devious writers say about politics as for the ways in which their work is political, and here is the rub. Ellmann's biography persuades us of Joyce's political neutrality and bogus socialism, while a careful study of his literary works, even when one accounts for irony, inevitably shows us a seriousness of political purpose.

To go further, we must consider Joyce's knowledge of anarchist and socialist thinkers and what he did with that knowledge. Better yet we should read these forgotten political works ourselves; short of that they are best described in Dominic Manganiello's *Joyce's Politics* and Robert Scholes' "x/y: Joyce and Modernist Ideology," an unpublished paper read at the Tenth International James Joyce Symposium in Copenhagen. Here we learn, among other things, about Guglielmo Ferrero, an important political thinker mentioned in only a few lines of *James Joyce*. Ellmann knew about him, of course, from his editing of the *Letters*.[32]

As expressed in his biography of Joyce, Ellmann's basic assumption about politics, if I judge aright, is that a political philosophy based on self-interest should not be taken seriously. But, alas, since most of us fall into that category, Ellmann's bemused perspective of Joyce's politics strikes an odd note: "They encouraged him in his feeling that socialism should come, for how else should he be fed? He needed a redistribution of wealth if he was to be a spendthrift" (*JJ2*, 142). Or consider this misleading statement:

But, like other revolutionaries, he fattened on opposition and grew thin and pale when treated with indulgence. Whenever his relations with his native land were in danger of improving, he was to find a new incident to solidify his intransigence and to reaffirm the rightness of his voluntary absence. (*JJ2*, 109)

Seduced by such endearing wit, few readers have cared to go beyond *James Joyce* for a closer look at Joyce's politics, so that we are just now discovering an important dimension beyond the charge of hypocrisy. Scholes has emphasized that, during about the first seven years of this century, Joyce was a committed socialist. He describes the brand of socialism in terms which Ellmann would know from the *Letters*: "In the years when Joyce gave his serious attention to politics, he favored a revolution that would suppress parliamentary government, expropriate the vast wealth of the Catholic Church (*Letters*, II, 165–166), punish the bourgeoisie, and emancipate the proletariat (*Letters*, II, 198)" (Scholes, 8). Ellmann's quip "socialism has rarely been defended so tortuously" (*JJ1*, 205), Scholes justifiably describes as a "laconic put-down" of Joyce's politics (Scholes, 10).

What has Scholes learned that Ellmann apparently chose not to see? For one thing he has found the source of that central image of *A Portrait*'s closure: Stephen's desire to "forge in the smithy of my soul the uncreated conscience of my race."[33] Stephen's curious statement of revolutionary, altruistic political commitment so at odds with the Nineties' aestheticism which threatens to turn him inward, Scholes has traced back to a passage in Ferrero's *L'Europa giovane*: "La vecchia leggenda del popolo è diventata sentimento vivo e realtà nella coscienza dei grandi rappresentanti della razza." (The old popular legend has become a living sentiment, a reality, in the consciousness of the great representatives of the race [Scholes' translation]).[34] This interesting discovery surely results in large part from Scholes' unwillingness to believe that the story of Joyce's politics ends with egotistical, self-serving pronouncements.[35] Ellmann's endearing wit, his ironic viewpoint and tone, have in this instance become dated, shopworn and misleading. (With little justice I once chided Manganiello for the opposite tendency, a failure to see the ridiculous in Joyce's politics.)

Though he was dissatisfied with Ellmann's treatment of Joyce's socialism in *James Joyce*, Empson in *Using Biography* sets his gunsight more on Hugh Kenner, whose *Dublin's Joyce* has taught a generation of readers to read irony into Stephen's grandiose posturing. He says "Kenner has long been inclined to take the mickey out of Stephen."[36] As we have seen, Ellmann is equally inclined to take the mickey out of Joyce, and here the implications are important: two of the greatest influences on Joyce criticism in this century, *James Joyce* and *Dublin's Joyce*, have convinced countless readers that the artist as a young man, in fiction and in life, was essentially an ironic pose. It follows, then, that the political and aesthetic positions expressed in Joyce's works, as in his life, were little more than the juvenile posturing of an egotistical bohemian artist. Although Ellmann and Kenner surely could not have foreseen the effect their two books were to have, that effect has been to play down the political dimension of Joyce's works, and to delay the sort of promising discoveries made by Scholes and Manganiello.

Ellmann himself was not distracted, for Chapter Three of *The Consciousness of Joyce* was devoted to politics.[37] There and in his two-page article "Joyce and Politics," he takes a rather different tack from that of his biography. The latter work begins: "The often repeated assumption that Joyce was indifferent to politics misrepresents him. It comes from the simplistic notion that politics means voting in elections."[38] The general view that Joyce was politically indifferent, self-serving, and aloof, is somewhat mitigated by his attempts to aid Jews (mostly friends of friends) fleeing Nazi Germany; but the origin of this commonly-held view, however defined, is not rooted in some naive assumption that being political means voting, but based almost entirely on Ellmann's biography and Joyce's letters. However, in this article Ellmann does say that "[Joyce] shows himself to be political in the substance and texture of his work," a thesis he effectively demonstrates.[39] It depends on one's view of biography whether or not Ellmann is found remiss in not making the same point in *James Joyce*—in hesitating to go beyond the anecdotal and documentary evidence for a closer look both at Joyce's reading in political philosophy (as he does in *The Consciousness of Joyce*), and at fictional strategies with political implications. Our age seems to demand closer scrutiny, for in some ways Joyce's readership has caught up with him.

THE REVISED EDITION (1982)

A major biography of a modern figure will inevitably omit details which only come to light after publication; corrections would normally appear in subsequent printings and, in a biography of the importance of Ellmann's, one would expect a revised edition. The new *James Joyce* contains some forty-five additional pages and eighty-seven new illustrations, but the chronological framework remains the same, with new material added where appropriate. There are more quotations from letters, more on the Irish writer's knowledge of Jung and Freud, and Joyce's autopsy report is printed.

In an article on the new edition, Ellmann surveyed the new material, emphasizing the more titillating bits.[40] While visiting Locarno in 1917, Joyce unsuccessfully attempted to lure into a liaison a young German medical doctor, Gertrude Kaempffer, sending her two letters which she apparently destroyed; Kaempffer did remember the content of one letter, which told of a woodsy walk with a nanny when Joyce was fourteen, and what he may have described as his first sexual experience. When the nanny excused herself to urinate, young Joyce "jiggled furiously" (*JJ2*, 418). The Joyce of 1917 may have expected voyeuristic jiggling to be the appropriate response to his letter. Voyeurism was certainly a motif in several of Joyce's works, especially in the "Nausicaa" episode of *Ulysses*, where Bloom ogles a younger Gertrude and jiggles.

Ellmann implies that Dr. Kaempffer is the sole origin for the name of Gerty McDowell, who so freely shows her undies to Bloom. A stronger case has been made for the heroine of Maria Cummins' *The Lamplighter* (1854), another Gerty, though Joyce may well have had both sources in mind.[41] The latter book was a major influence on the prose style of "Nausicaa." Ellmann doubtless knows this, but gives no reason for preferring Kaempffer over Cummins; one suspects that the preference might derive from a desire to elevate in importance a "discovery" which might otherwise give evidence of little more than Joyce's rather cautious philandering, a weakness already well documented. The Kaempffer episode is, after all, the most interesting part of the new material in the revised edition.

Similarly dubious is Ellmann's willingness to accept Joyce's word that Frank Budgen, a sculptor's model and sometime sailor, was Joyce's model for the old salt W. B. Murphy in "Eumaeus," an idea for which no solid evidence is supplied. The resemblance is anything but striking, but it makes a good story.

Ellmann's article (in the *New York Times Book Review*) describes other new material in the revised edition. There are new letters to Joyce from Harriet Weaver containing more precise evidence of her generosity. Among the new photographs is one of Henry Carr, the Zurich consular official with whom Joyce had litigation, in Black Watch uniform. (Tom Stoppard made him a character in his play *Travesties*.) We also have a new story from Joyce's sister Margaret: she and James watched for their mother's ghost, which she claims to have seen in brown habit at midnight. In "Circe," Stephen has a hallucination of his mother, decayed and in graveclothes. A priest at Joyce's old school Clongowes found a punishment book which lists Joyce as having been pandied more than once for various infractions of the rules, which sets him rather apart from the martyred Stephen. Newly published correspondence from Lady Gregory, Synge and Oliver Gogarty add to our knowledge of the younger Joyce, and the implications of Joyce's Padua examinations as well as his Trieste library are noted. There is more information on Samuel Beckett's unwilling involvement with Joyce's daughter Lucia, though still not as much as one finds in Deirdre Bair's biography of Beckett.[42] More material on Joyce's flirtation with Marthe Fleischmann has been added, and also a dream notebook by Joyce. We will debate the importance of this material, but beyond dispute is the excellence of Mary Reynolds' exhaustive new index to the revised edition.

Most pages of the new edition seem to contain changes in wording, and there are many more reference notes. Charles Peake spotted some 300 corrections, alterations and insertions, though he objects that where Ellmann has changed his mind he does not satisfy our curiosity about the reasons.[43] Philip Gaskell concluded from a survey of the new material that since none of it changes Ellmann's view of Joyce in any significant way, what we have is not a new edition, but rather an enlarged one.[44] (On this point Peake disagrees.)

Ellmann's handling of the *Letters* and *Giacomo Joyce*, an issue we shall discuss below, makes it necessary to enquire into any commercial objectives that may have warranted the publication of a revised edition of *James Joyce* in 1982. The occasion was obviously the centenary of Joyce's birth, but the question is— was 1982 a deadline which in any way caused the revisions to be rushed or truncated?

LIMITATIONS OF THE REVISED EDITION

About the first edition, Kristian Smidt says:

> Above all it would have been interesting to see more of Joyce in the actual process of writing: the dedicated artist in the smithy of his soul, the literary craftsman putting his thoughts down on paper. What were his habits? How did he use his notes, how concentrate, how write? These are questions which Ellmann answers almost parenthetically or not at all,

and they are too important in the biography of a great writer to be so summarily dismissed.[45]

This deficiency was not addressed in the revised edition. Consequently it could be argued that, in the interest of a wider readership and of a better story, Ellmann has to some extent emphasized the seediness, improvidence and quirkiness of the man Joyce at the expense of images which would shape our view of Joyce the creator. As at *JJ2*, p. 75, Ellmann's tendency is to catalog books Joyce read rather than describe their impact, which became the subject of his later book *The Consciousness of Joyce*.

An anonymous reviewer of the first edition said: "Yet it had been a life of intense effort and achievement. The grandeur is somehow absent from Mr. Ellmann's record."[46] That grandeur becomes visible in the creative process that gave us works like *Ulysses* and *Finnegans Wake*, about which, despite complaints about the biography's length, more could have been revealed. Considerably more could have been said about the Paris years and the evolution of *Finnegans Wake*. Since the publication of the first edition of *James Joyce*, there has appeared a lengthy checklist of publications on Joyce's artistic process as well as editions of notes and drafts of his works. In 1980 the massive *James Joyce Archive* appeared in sixty-three volumes.[47] All this evidence of Joyce's creativity has been largely ignored in the biography while, one could argue, too much has been made of Gertrude Kaempffer and Marthe Fleischmann. When discussing Joyce's ludicrously inept translation of plays by Gerhart Hauptmann (*JJ2*, 87–88), surely it could be revealed that one of those translations has been published.[48] How strange also to see in a work published in 1982 a reference to the 1941 Slocum and Cahoon bibliography of Joyce (*JJ2*, 746). It does not seem too much to ask that a revised biography of one of the century's greatest writers reveal more about his creative process. One could also wish Ellmann had profited more from the major Joyce criticism published since 1959 rather than relying primarily on his own critical insights; but some would contend that this is beyond the task of biography, revised or not.

ELLMANN THE EDITOR

Near universal admiration among readers for Ellmann's *James Joyce* has been mixed with consternation at his editorial decisions that seem to have been prompted more by expectations of commercial gain than by conscientious scholarly reasons. After Stuart Gilbert edited *The Letters of James Joyce*,[49] many more letters turned up. Ellmann then published two more volumes in 1966, but instead of integrating the first volume into the chronological scheme of a new three-volume edition, he simply published two more volumes which contain letters, early to late. The Gilbert edition was reissued as Volume I. Those who use the letters are obliged to search the indexes of both the first and third volumes, but normally it will not occur to an inexperienced user to search further than the index in Volume III. A few dollars were saved, but considerable confusion was caused, especially among students. Would Stuart Gilbert really have objected to the volumes being integrated as long as he was listed as an editor?

Another problem with the three volumes of *Letters* was that, presumably in deference to Joyce's heirs, the notoriously obscene letters of 1909 from Joyce to his wife Nora were omitted. Unfortunately for the family, Stanislaus Joyce (or his widow) sold rather than destroyed them after his brother's death. The letters may have been too strong a dose for readers in 1966, but presumably not for those of 1975, for in that year Ellmann turned a delicate situation to advantage by publishing the *Selected Letters of James Joyce*.[50] On the cover we read "The editor's choice of the best letters from James Joyce's three great volumes, with important additions of previously unpublished letters." Since the *Selected Letters of James Joyce* seemed primarily intended to publish mysterious letters, which students of Joyce had for decades been perusing in the Cornell University Library, doubtless many people snickered at the claim that these were "the best" that Joyce had written.

Joyce's grandson Stephen Joyce has complained bitterly about unsavory revelations concerning his grandparents in the biography and published letters, but he should be somewhat appeased that Ellmann did not use the occasion of a revised edition of *James Joyce* to analyze or quote in greater detail the letters of 1909. Denis Donoghue, on the other hand, has said that this omission was highly regrettable, and showed the revised edition to be lacking in suitable candor. He remembered Ellmann's statement that "we ask of biographers the same candour that our novelists have taught us to accept from them" (*Golden Codgers*, 2–3).[51]

Another apparently cynical decision, seemingly intended to capitalize on the success of *James Joyce*, was the publication of *Giacomo Joyce* as a separate volume in slip case.[52] This notebook, in Joyce's careful calligraphy, celebrates his passion for a young woman whom he was tutoring in English. Written in Trieste in 1914, it could have been the subject of a fine article. But the sixteen-page book (with plenty of blank space) accompanied by a manuscript facsimile, was very expensive. One would have thought that the modernist equivalent of the Dead Sea Scrolls had been found, for the slim volume was announced on the front page of the *New York Times* and elsewhere as a major manuscript discovery.

If seen in this light, the publication of *Giacomo Joyce* was misleading, for the juicier parts of the notebook had already been quoted in Ellmann's *James Joyce*. There the object of Joyce's passion was positively identified as Amalia Popper (*JJ1*, 353). In his introduction to *Giacomo Joyce*, though, Ellmann plays the tease or suffers from memory lapse when it comes to naming Popper: "A love poem which is never recited, [the notebook] is Joyce's attempt at the sentimental education of a dark lady" (ix). Now we have a mystery of Shakespearean importance, front page news. In the revised edition of *James Joyce* Ellmann changed his view: "This may well have been Amalia Popper" (*JJ2*, 342). Joyce would have delighted in all this hocus-pocus.

Criticizing Ellmann's biography of Joyce, as some of us have done, can hardly dent its greatness, for we are like a few small mice nibbling around a royal wedding cake. Although it would be possible to compile a small catalogue of its imperfections, there would be general disagreement about what it should contain. We will probably never be able to replace any major element of the portrait with a competing image. Horace Reynolds said it well: "Many have long known how remarkable was Joyce's work. How remarkable he was as a man was never fully known before Mr. Ellmann's distinguished biography."[53] Joyce himself may have said it even better in the last stanza of his "Epilogue to Ibsen's 'Ghosts'"':

> Nay more, were I not all I was,
> Weak, wanton, waster out and out,
> There would have been no world's applause
> And damn all to write home about.[54]

CHAPTER SIX

George Painter's
Marcel Proust

JEFFREY MEYERS

I

George Painter's biography of Proust grew out of a lifelong fascination with *Remembrance of Things Past*. And his own Proustian parody idealizes his origins and describes an early epiphany: "I was born [in 1914] in Birmingham, an unreal city in the English Midlands, ugly and black to outsiders, but to natives and exiles beautiful and haunting, navel of the labyrinth of place and time. Wandering alone in a public park there at the age of six towards a dead tree which I never reached, I had a moment of vision, a sense of personal identity and the reality beyond appearances, that marked me for life."[1]

His father was a musician, singer and schoolmaster; his mother an artist; and his parents gave him reading, solitude and holidays in the West Country. Painter said: "I've been interested in Proust since my school days, first read him when I was 14 and in search of literature in the local public library in Birmingham. I was browsing through the shelves and saw *Swann's Way*, and something attracted me about the title. I took the book and was immediately bowled over and have gone on reading and thinking about Proust, and in the end writing about him, ever since."[2]

Painter's preparation for his eventual career as a biographer was scholarly and archival. He was educated at King Edward's School, Birmingham, and at Trinity College, Cambridge. A brilliant student, Painter won three scholarships and three prizes, and graduated with first class honors in both parts of the Classical Tripos. He taught Latin for a year at Liverpool

University before joining the Department of Printed Books at the British Museum in 1938. He married his cousin in 1942, had two daughters and served in the army from October 1941 until July 1946. In 1954 he became Assistant Keeper in charge of ten thousand fifteenth-century printed books, the largest and finest collection of incunabula in the world: "They needed a classical scholar because so much of it would be medieval Latin, and they chose me, rightly or wrongly, and I did that for twenty years."[3] His training in Classics—with its close attention to the text, interest in factual details and careful sifting of evidence—influenced his approach to biographical research. His Classics masters taught Painter "to read and write both Latin and Greek, for the sheer pleasure of discovering and experiencing, and reconstructing and reliving the ancient writer from the writing, the individual from his world." He learned to view biography as a process "of finding evidence and trying to express what seemed to be its meaning in a context of human life."[4]

Though Painter's professional life was scholarly, he felt his talents were also artistic. In 1951, at the age of thirty-seven, he published *The Road to Sinodun* [near Dorchester]: *A Winter and Summer Monodrama*, a volume of poems written during 1940–41 "in plain English that rhymed and scanned," which were influenced by the bitterly ironic mode of Housman and Eliot. They did not attract much attention, sold about forty copies and brought in royalties of less than two pounds. He then realized that "the creations, minds, and lives of my favourite writers were . . . far more interesting to me than my own; and most interesting of all was the mysterious relationship between these creations and these minds and lives."[5] Painter's true vocation turned out to be biography: a literary form that combines the drudgery of research with the excitement of the chase and attempts to probe the mystery of artistic creation.

Painter, an extraordinarily learned man, is an authority in four fields: Classics, incunabula, medieval history and cartography, and French literature. He has translated André Gide's two satirical novels, *Marshlands* and *Prometheus Misbound* (1953), Marcel Proust's *Letters to His Mother* (1956) and André Maurois's *The Chelsea Way; or, Marcel in England: A Proustian Parody* (1967); produced a scholarly study (with R. A. Skelton and T. E. Marston), *The Vinland Map and The Tartar Relation*

(1965) and *Studies in Fifteenth-Century Printing* (1984); and published four biographies: *André Gide* (1951), *Marcel Proust* (1959, 1965), *William Caxton* (1976) and the first of three projected volumes on *Chateaubriand* (1977).

Painter has remarked that his book about a lifelong invalid was conceived, appropriately enough, when he was ill: "During a bout of influenza in 1947 I first read a volume of Proust's letters, and found in them the very people and situations in his actual life that reappear transformed to the level of high art in *A la recherche du temps perdu*. . . . I resolved to write his biography in order to explain him to myself, little knowing that the task would demand eighteen years: six of preliminary research and thinking, and twelve of writing."[6]

Painter has explained why the gestation period was unusually long: "Work at the British Museum was arduous and exacting, a 42-hour, 5½-day week with 36 days annual leave, and it would have been neither possible nor legitimate to write there, or even read. . . . I worked or wrote in the evenings, at weekends, on holiday, at mealbreaks, while commuting in the train, all the time I could, from five minutes to all day, very slowly, very painfully, averaging nothing, or a sentence, or a paragraph."[7] He has also confessed: "I write with torture, and it's probably a self-punishment," and has described the biographer—not the subject—as a sacrificial victim: "Biography is often thought of as the vampire art—the vampire feeding upon his subject. For me it's the exact opposite. My subject has fed upon me. He's taken my life-blood while I've tried to give him life. I've sacrificed my own life, I've sacrificed my personality, and I've done it willingly."[8]

Painter won the Duff Cooper Prize for the second volume of *Proust* and the James Tait Black Prize for his life of Chateaubriand—a "great invisible presence" in Proust's novel. He was elected Fellow of the Royal Society of Literature in 1965 and awarded an honorary doctorate by Edinburgh University in 1979. He has lived in Hove, on the Channel coast near Brighton, since 1970; and calls himself reclusive and unsociable ("my friends are all dead").[9]

II

Painter first expressed in *André Gide* his fundamental principle of biography: his belief that the life-writer must treat the works as a part of, not a supplement to, his subject's life. And he elaborated his biographical principles in two important interviews: with Simon Blow in the *Guardian* (1977) and with Phyllis Grosskurth (the biographer of J. A. Symonds and Havelock Ellis) in *Salmagundi* (1983).

In his Foreword to *Gide* Painter declared: "no one so far has attempted to describe the actual nature and content of his work, and to show its organic growth from the history of his mind and heart. Before the work of a great writer can be appreciated as a whole, it must be seen as an evolutionary sequence from his first book to his last, and its relationship (hidden, but essential and organic) with the man himself must be restored."[10] Gide's works, like Proust's, are essentially autobiographical and developed directly from his personal experience. So a consideration of his works has to be integrated with a discussion of his life in order to reveal their significant interrelationship. The works of art justify the investigation of the life, which in turn illuminates the works and makes us value them more highly. Painter's particular contribution to modern biography is his scholarly skill in re-creating the sources of the novel in order to reveal or come close to the creative act itself. Whereas most biographers seek to discover living informants to ascertain the facts, Painter emphasizes an imaginative grasp of Proust's novel through searching and sifting the elemental components of the text.

Painter illustrates the "organic relationship" of Proust's life and art by showing how the young amateur, dilettante, flatterer and snob, who frequented luxury hotels, great restaurants and society drawing-rooms, was transformed into the magnanimous, reclusive and brilliant novelist. His biographical research directly informs our understanding of the novel because all the facts, episodes and characters in the life have their parallel in the novel. Painter shows how Proust's genius evolved from his early works—*Pleasures and Days*, *Jean Santeuil*, the Ruskin translations and *Contre Sainte-Beuve*—at the same time that he discovered the technique of unconscious memory.

Proust cultivated this technique—paradoxically triggered by

the banal act of dipping a piece of sponge cake into a cup of tea—in order to focus his creative imagination on the reality he had experienced. Through the great theme of Time Regained, the novel's art redeemed the chaotic nature of experience and distilled it into an intelligible and beautiful form. The ritual of the *madeleine* became, for Proust, the missing key: "it was reality itself, freed from the mask of time and habit, 'a fragment of pure life preserved in its purity, which we can only know when it is so preserved, because, in the moment when we live it, it is not present to our memory but surrounded by sensations which suppress it.' "[11]

Painter believes that biography is now "the most living literary art form," for like the novel it reaches a wide audience and exerts a powerful cultural influence by portraying the struggles and achievements of literary heroes. He states that he writes biography "because I read it and most of all feel the necessity for it when I'm reading my favourite writers." The urge to read and to write biography comes from an intuitive grasp of the life between the lines, from a desire to know *more* about the cultural milieu in which the work of art was created. He adopted as his literary models three long, sometimes multi-volumed, exhaustively researched and elegantly written biographies: Ernest Jones' *Freud* (1953–57), Leslie Marchand's *Byron* (1957) and Richard Ellmann's *Joyce* (1959). "I don't think any biography had any direct influence on mine in style or method," he explains, "except that reading in 1939 Steegmuller's *Flaubert and Madame Bovary* and in 1940 Newman White's *Shelley*, long before I ever thought of becoming a practitioner, left the lessons that biography could be live and entertaining (Steegmuller) and large in scale (White), and helped me to want mine to be both."[12] He justly feels that his own book has had a certain influence "in the approach to [large-scale] biography and the increase of interest in biography in the last twenty years." "In great works of art," Painter concludes, "human life is being expressed at a deeper, more intense, more clear-sighted level than anything we can achieve ourselves. That's why we write biographies."[13]

Unlike most biographers, Painter never read anyone else on his subject and denied himself one of the great pleasures of research by scrupulously avoiding anyone who had ever known Proust. One of his fundamental principles is the need "to work entirely from primary sources. . . . Letters, documents, reminiscences, memoirs certainly, but they've got to be used critically because people don't remember properly. . . . [But] you must never believe anything you read in print when you're writing a biography."[14] He used only written evidence but felt that evidence was not enough, and brought his subject back to life with fact fired by his imagination: "You've got to see the connections, to see it as it's happening in real life, and not just as a literary abstraction."[15]

Painter even declared, rather perversely, that he would not have liked to know the people who lived in Proust's world, that "if somebody had said, 'Proust's calling this evening, do look in and meet him,' I wouldn't have wanted to. I wouldn't have turned my head to see him across the street. . . . [He couldn't] tell me anything . . . which I wouldn't find much more intensely, acceptably and deeply in [his] works." Though he met, for example, Marthe Bibesco and Violet Schiff, he maintained: "I've never, practically never, obtained information by word of mouth, and usually when I've done so, I've regretted it. It turned out to be quite incorrect. . . . All the people who could have told me anything had already put it into print, some of them many times over."[16]

Painter identified with his subject in terms of his method and his artistic approach. Like Proust, he seeks to imagine rather than simply find the facts in a journalistic fashion. By avoiding the people who had actually known Proust, by refusing to hear how a friend felt about an incident Proust has described, he remains completely loyal to the Proustian vision. Painter's biography, an elaborate critical reading of Proust's long novel, is illuminating in the same way as the novel is. It belongs with Ellmann's *Joyce* and Douglas Day's *Malcolm Lowry*—lives of authors of one great work which the biography helps to elucidate.

Painter's belief that recollection is more significant than actual experience is closely connected to the central theme of Proust's novel, the recovery of the past through memory, and to the central technique. For "just as the Japanese amuse themselves by filling a porcelain bowl with water and steeping in it little crumbs of paper which until then are without character or form," so, through Painter's act of creation as well as evocation, intangible people "take on colour and distinctive shape, become ... permanent and recognisable ... [and assuming] their proper shapes and growing solid, spring into being" (I.36).

But Painter's position is somewhat paradoxical. Though he believes "it's the biographer's duty to get inside that mind and live the life of that subject," he retains a profound scepticism about his ability to get inside the minds of Proust's surviving friends. Like Proust, Painter feels his vision will be sharper and imagination stronger if he remains aloof. As an invalid whose asthmatic attacks led to moments of intense pain and exhaustion; as a Jew and Dreyfusard pardoning rebuffs and flattered by condescension; as a homosexual doomed to constant duplicity and obliged to make a secret of his life; and as a writer whose great work, by its very existence, profaned his mother while it triumphantly vindicated his dedication to art, Proust, with all his worldliness and charm, also stood clearly outside the society he portrayed and anatomized with such subtlety and perception.

Though scrupulous in its factual research and textual analysis, Painter's view of biography is novelistic. He believes the life-writer follows the same process as the fiction-writer, and knows by instinct how to convey the passage of time and when to end the book: "the artist has creative imagination, the artistic biographer has recreative imagination. You look at your evidence and your facts and their relationships, and they begin to come alive. ... We live our lives hour by hour, day by day, and you've got to produce the feeling of day to day living, of this slow and sometimes very rapid movement in the texture of your book. ... You have your solution to which you're applying all these ingredients, and there comes a point when the solution is saturated, when the law of diminishing returns comes, when you feel this is enough to get this thing right. Then you stop."[17]

III

The biographical principles expressed in the Foreword to *Gide* and in the retrospective interviews with Simon Blow and Phyllis Grosskurth were arrogantly and categorically stated (rather than carefully argued) in the Preface to the first volume of *Marcel Proust: A Biography* (1959). The Preface laid the intellectual and aesthetic foundations of this work, but the dogmatic tone provoked the hostility of a number of critics. Painter later acknowledged that the Preface was a contentious challenge and a strategic error (and did not write a Preface to the second volume of *Proust* or to *Chateaubriand*). As he told Grosskurth: "I was a very naughty young man [i.e., age 45] to use such words and I probably wouldn't do it now. I must say that sometimes, when I read the preface, I don't altogether like the tone of it."[18]

But he also defended the Preface and declared: "It was an indispensable manifesto, historically necessitated by the then state of thought or *idées reçues* on literary biography or Proust, and I think it did its work, angered only those whom the cap fitted or those who cannot bear to be told things they don't think already, and has been generally assimilated whether directly or indirectly to the point of seeming obvious and axiomatic (it was both to me when I wrote it), instead of paradoxical and heretical."[19]

Though Painter claims his biography is "not intended as a controversial work," he recklessly abandons the scholar's false humility and debt to his predecessors, and announces that "the subject has never yet been treated with anything approaching scholarly method"—that is, with exhaustive research based on a carefully conceived theory of biography. He also defiantly declares: "I have endeavoured to write a definitive biography of Proust: a complete, exact and detailed narrative of his life, that is, based on every known or discoverable primary source, and on primary sources only. . . . I think I may claim that something like nine-tenths of the narrative here given is new to Proustian biography, or conversely that previous biographers have used only about one-tenth of the discoverable sources." Though Painter stresses his objective scholarly method, the most striking characteristic of the biography is the imaginative range and psychological depth. Painter's unhappily phrased claim that ninety percent of his material is new cannot be verified and is doubtless exaggerated. He must have meant, by this assertion, that the meaning he has invested in the material and the interpretation he gives to the facts—if not the actual facts themselves—are entirely new.

Painter next attacks "one of the dogmas of Proustian criticism, that his novel can and must be treated as a closed system" and read entirely without reference to Proust's biography and background. In opposition to this dogma, he reiterates his belief that "no aspect of Proust or his work . . . can be studied without an accurate and detailed knowledge of his life." Anticipating attacks on this point, he adds: "I hope those who judge . . . my work will consider whether the facts are true, rather than whether the critical approach demanded by the facts happens to be fashionable at the present moment."[20]

Painter's Preface then considers the vital question of the relation between Proust's art and life ("one of the chief meanings of Time Regained"), mentions his attempt to identify all the originals or components that were fused into Proust's people and places ("though he invented nothing, he altered everything"), and reveals his obsessive desire to connect every aspect of the novel to factual reality. "By discovering which aspects of his originals he chose or rejected," Painter observes, "how he combined many models into each new figure, and most of all how he altered material reality to make it conform more closely to symbolic reality, we can observe the workings of his imagination at the very moment of creation. . . . *A la recherche* turns out to be not only based entirely on his own experiences: it is intended to be the symbolic story of his life . . . it is not, properly speaking, a fiction, but a creative autobiography" (I.xii–xiii). Painter's method is to find the factual source for every aspect of the novel. And his biography emphasizes the factual basis by providing two separate indexes: the first of real persons and places, the second of fictitious characters and places in Proust's novel; and by cross-referencing each index to the other.

It is ironic that even the most sober aspects of Painter's Preface—his discussion of the bibliography, references and citations to Proust's work—provide points of contention. For he states that they would not appear in the first volume and would be postponed until the second, in order to prevent rival scholars from appropriating his sources and rushing into print before he could complete his work. "To avoid needless repetition," Painter writes, "—and also, I confess, to avoid laying all my cards on the table before the game is finished [though he certainly has done this in the Preface]—I have postponed giving a full bibliography of the sources used, together with detailed references for each statement, till the second and final volume, which will appear in two years' time." Painter concludes that "it seemed imperative to give references to the standard *Pléiade* edition of the original text in three volumes" (I.xv) rather than to the superb English translation by C. K. Scott-Moncrieff— though the difficult French text would scarcely serve the needs of the "general reader" to whom Painter addressed his book.

IV

When the first volume of *Marcel Proust* was published, many of the critics concentrated on the Preface rather than on the book and disputed Painter's controversial assertions: that previous scholarship was worthless (it is difficult to see how Painter could dismiss his predecessors if he had never read anyone else on his subject), that his biography was definitive, that nine-tenths of the narrative was new, that Proust's "creative autobiography" could not be understood without a knowledge of his life, that Proust "invented nothing," that every aspect of the book was based on reality, that all the fictional characters could be connected to their multiple original models, that no scholarly sources would be given in the first volume and that the French rather than the English edition of the novel would be cited in the notes. Publishing the biography in two volumes instead of one was a serious mistake, for it aroused expectations that could not be gratified for several years and diminished the impact of the entire book.

Critics recognized and praised Painter's solid scholarship, lucid interpretations, powerful prose style and penetrating portrayal of Proust as a flawed but heroic figure. But his "heretical" belief that "biography is an essential and preliminary part of criticism"[21] came into conflict with the prevailing theories of New Criticism—associated with the writings of I. A. Richards, T. S. Eliot and John Crowe Ransom—which held that works of art should be treated independently of the biography and intentions of the author, and of the social conditions at the time of its production. The fallacy of this view, of course, was that critics attempting to treat the work of art as a closed system were perfectly aware of the social and biographical background and used this knowledge, intentionally or not, when formulating their critique of the novel. Painter played a significant role in leading readers away from the once stimulating but ultimately sterile strictures of the New Criticism.

The English novelists who reviewed the first volume were much more sympathetic than the American critics and scholars. Painter's attempt "to bring [Proust's] friends and acquaintances to life as they were when he knew them" was praised by L. P. Hartley. Writing in the *Spectator* (October 16, 1959), he admired the complete evocation of Proust's society and felt that it *was* the definitive biography of the author and companion to the novel. In an early review in the *New Statesman* (September 19, 1959), Pamela Hansford Johnson, who had contributed an essay to Painter's edition of Proust's *Letters to His Mother* in 1956, called it "the finest biography of our time" and emphasized its blend of "intensive scholarship, imaginative sympathy, love and cool thinking." In the *Observer* (September 20, 1959), Angus Wilson, who had been Painter's colleague at the British Museum, pronounced it "brilliant and scholarly." He particularly valued the "depiction of place and people, his revelation of the raw material for the novel." The review in the *Daily Telegraph* by Anthony Powell, whose multi-volumed *Dance to the Music of Time* was profoundly influenced by Proust, concluded: "Mr. Painter has done his work so well that it is hard to speak in moderate terms of his skill and unobtrusive wit."

The reviewers in American journals (outside the English old-boy network) recognized Painter's merits but were far more critical of his biographical approach and arrogant claims. The drama critic Richard Gilman, writing in the Catholic weekly, *Commonweal* (October 16, 1959), questioned the biographical premises but commended Painter's scholarship, acknowledged that he had identified all the originals and agreed that he had, as he claimed, achieved the definitive biography. Gilman wondered, however, if Painter could deliver what he had promised in the second volume. In the *Yale Review* (December 1959), the excellent French scholar, W. H. Frohock, said "Painter's industry and learning are admirable." But he criticized Painter's "arrogantly assumed omniscience"; and stated that much of the material was quite familiar, and nine-tenths of it was certainly *not* new.

Two of the American reviews were particularly negative. In the *New York Herald Tribune Book Review* (August 16, 1959), Marvin Lowenthal, editor of Montaigne's *Autobiography*, agreed with Frohock that the new material was indeed familiar, perversely claimed that André Maurois and Richard Barker give "a far more vivid picture" of Proust, and called Painter's richly detailed volume "a singularly padded and jerky biography" which "constantly relapses into . . . a Handbook to Proust." The most antagonistic review came in the *Nation* (October 3, 1959) from Mina Curtiss, translator and editor of the *Letters of Marcel Proust* (1949), who seemed to resent the invasion of her scholarly territory and to express a personal grudge. She mentioned some unpublished material that had not been used by Painter and maintained that only one-tenth of the material was new. She disputed Painter's facts, felt he had demeaned the power of Proust's imagination by linking it to actual events, called his work a series of "defective detective stories," and claimed that he lacked the humility and love that she presumably possessed.[22]

In the Preface of 1959 Painter had promised that detailed references would be given in the second volume, "which will appear in two years' time." In the fourth impression of the first volume (1965), he changed this to "six years' time" in order to match the publication of the second volume. During their interview, Grosskurth remarked: "when you published the first volume of *Proust* in 1959, you said that Volume Two would appear six years later." Painter, overcome by vanity (or perhaps by faulty memory), replied: "Did I now? That was a very good guess." And Grosskurth naively agreed: "You did, and it appeared exactly six years later."[23]

The reviews of the second volume were even more enthusiastic and vituperative than those of the first. Critics who admired the book praised the new interpretation of the material; those who disliked it either resented the mass of detail or the darker, more complex picture of Proust which interfered with their preconceived view of the writer. The literary critic John Gross, in *Encounter* (October 1965), felt the second half of Proust's life was less interesting, but that Painter "has sifted the evidence scrupulously, and rearranged an unwieldy mass of materials with admirable clarity. . . . In a word, he is indispensable." The philosopher Stuart Hampshire, writing in the *New Statesman* (July 9, 1965), perceived that Proust's "art was rooted in his own pathological condition." Hampshire felt that the second volume, which subordinated biography to the composition of the novel, "will be found slightly disappointing, as if there had been some loss of confidence in the interval; the detached, assured tone is gone." This change may have occurred because Painter had been attacked by certain critics, had come to regret the tone of the Preface to the first volume and had taken much longer than anticipated to complete the second.

The critics in America were generally harsher in their judgments than the English. On the front page of the *New York Times Book Review* (November 7, 1965), the distinguished English biographer, Peter Quennell, commented that Painter "attaches too much importance to Proust's relations with his mother" (though this was one of the most convincing aspects of the book); but agreed with his fellow-countrymen that the life illuminated the work: "I have seldom read a biography that provides so convincing an account of how a masterpiece evolves." The most intelligent review was written on the front page of the *Washington Post Book Week* (November 7, 1965) by a leading American Proust scholar, Roger Shattuck. He said the book was "organized in clusters around the crucial moments in Proust's life . . . [and] backed by Painter's psychological perceptiveness and sturdy prose style." Shattuck called it "a great biography" that achieves "a new level of accuracy and understanding, and stands in its own right as a work of art." In the *New York Review of Books* (November 11, 1965), Anne de Colleyre, a French poet and critic of Proust, noted Painter's cast of mind and psychological penetration: "Painter is a snob, as were Stendhal and Baudelaire, and his snobbishness provides him not only with a biased view of French history but also a remarkable literary insight." And she convincingly concluded: "It is a major biography in English, distinguished by thorough scholarship, honesty in acknowledging the frailty of genius, and a cogent style."

In the *Virginia Quarterly Review* (Winter 1966), Milton Hindus, author of *The Proustian Vision* (1954) and *A Reader's Guide to Marcel Proust* (1962), felt the need to defend Proust against Painter's methodology and unwelcome revelations about Proust's character. Hindus upheld the New Critics' viewpoint, denied that everything in the novel was based on Proust's own experience and objected to Painter's thesis that the work could not be fully understood without a knowledge of Proust's life. But Hindus' critical point was not a vital issue. Since Proust's novel, his fictional manifestation of reality, was utterly convincing, it did not greatly matter whether Proust had transformed or invented experience. Hindus also disliked the "pretentious style" (which everyone else had admired), and (like Marvin Lowenthal) rather perversely insisted that Richard Barker's superficial biography of 1958 was superior. Unable to bear the truth about his idol or accept the frailty of genius, Hindus attacked Painter's "voyeuristic fascination with the most intimate details of his private life."

In July 1960, just after the publication of the first volume, Marie Riefstahl-Nordlinger, an English friend who had introduced Proust to Ruskin and helped him translate the Master's work, attacked Painter in a cruelly wounding article. It had been originally broadcast on November 1, 1959 over the French Service of the BBC and then reprinted, disguised as a review, in *X*, a short-lived London quarterly. Though Riefstahl-Nordlinger tried to undermine Painter's authority by listing a series of minor factual errors, she was actually attempting to discredit his fundamental principles of biography, to dispute his right to gain access to intimate information and to question the entire point of his enterprise. She was even more possessive and proprietary about Proust than Curtiss and Hindus; and, like them, self-righteously felt that she alone was the sole repository of truth about her idol. Painter's quarrel with Riefstahl-Nordlinger is important because it reveals the resistance of the old guard to the new purpose and method of biography: to illuminate the artist's imagination by utilizing every available piece of evidence. Painter easily won the argument, partly because the points at issue were trivial, mainly because Riefstahl-Nordlinger, ostensibly disputing factual details, never directly addressed the much more serious issues that had originally inspired her outburst.

In a dignified and persuasive response in *X* in October 1960, Painter reiterated his admiration (fully expressed in his book) for his unexpected adversary; answered in considerable detail some fourteen trivial points "on which Mme. Riefstahl-Nordlinger accuses me of inaccuracy, negligence, misrepresentation, ignorance, malice, invention, mistranslation and prying"; and stated: "I can find no justification, in the factual objections which she makes to this small fraction of my work, for her imputations against my integrity, my scholarship and my taste." Invoking the recent example of Ellmann's *Joyce*, Painter strongly objected to Riefstahl-Nordlinger's assertion

that "biography is a rather dubious business," and concluded
with a fundamental principle of his work: "I am staggered by
her remarks that an attempt 'to observe the workings of Proust's
imagination' (surely one of the primary duties of the biographer,
and one for which she herself has given invaluable evidence)
can appeal 'only to the clinically minded.' "[24]

The dispute with Riefstahl-Nordlinger was revived and
publicized, after the review of the second volume appeared in
the *Times Literary Supplement*, when John Lehmann defended his
distant cousin's little known attack on Painter. In the *Times
Literary Supplement* of August 19, 1965, Painter responded to
Lehmann's "ignorant and baseless smear" with a magnificently
persuasive defense: "I answered the fourteen factual points with
which she backed her imputations on my integrity as a scholar,
showing that in most she was mistaken and I was right; in
some I had relied on her own previous words, which she then
clarified or retracted; others were matters of opinion, based in
my case on evidence; but none involved the validity of any
important conclusion, still less of my good faith."[25] The
astonishing aspect of all these contradictory reviews is not that
Painter's work received its just praise, but that it also provoked,
from supposedly qualified critics, such violent and self-interested
abuse.

V

Painter explains that the first volume of *Marcel Proust*—which
concludes with the death of Proust's father in 1903—analyzes
the autobiographical material used in the novel and that "a
discussion of his methods of synthesis will appear in the second
volume" (I.xii). Painter places the vast quantity of material in
its organic order, and maintains the narrative thrust of the
story through four long but necessary digressions: on the
topography of the symbolic landscape, Illiers (chapter 2), on
Proust's hosts, hostesses and acquaintances in society (chapter
10), on the Dreyfus affair (chapter 13) and on Proust's study of
Ruskin (chapter 14). Painter links the thematic clusters of the
narrative by means of clear transitions: "It is time for a further
glimpse of Montesquiou," "It is time to tell the strange story of
the Vinteuil Septet" (II.5, 242). His style is lucid, leisurely and

elegant; with a rich particularity of detail (though he could have been more precise about what Proust's circle ate and drank at their memorable banquets) and a fine dramatic flair.

The span of Proust's life (1871–1922) extends from the Franco-Prussian War till after the Great War. Painter, with an impressive mastery of the background, places his subject in the social, political and cultural context. He vividly re-creates, for example, the disasters that occurred when the Seine overflowed its banks in the summer of 1910, which led to renovations in Proust's building, prolonged attacks of asthma and interruptions in his work: "The bears in the Jardin des Plantes were rescued in imminent danger of drowning; it was feared that the crocodiles might escape from their flooded pools; and the poor giraffe had to be left, knee-deep, to die of exposure. Sewers burst in the streets, or rose hideously in cellars, and rats fled through the boulevards" (II.158).

Painter's "palace of pleasure" exhibits a Proustian fascination with society (as well as a tendency to overload the narrative with lists of titles and proper nouns): "In their drawing-rooms flourished a gay elegance, a fantastic individuality, a chivalrous freedom, a living interplay of minds, morals and emotions" (II.315). Like Proust himself, Painter loves the definitive epigram and is fond of recording witty *mots*. Léon Daudet said: "I wouldn't have trusted [the surgeon] to cut my hair"; a cocotte "first posed in tights and spangles at the Théâtre du Châtelet, then put on more clothes to become an actress, and lastly took everything off to be an artist's model" (I.101, 217). He reveals how Proust transformed the dross of the frequently empty, heartless and corrupt society into the gold of literature, and made those people appear more interesting in fiction than they ever were in reality.

Painter portrays all the major characters in Proust's life with subtlety and vividness, and painstakingly unravels the strands of his personal relationships. Charles Haas, the model for Charles Swann, was, he said, "the only Jew ever to be accepted by Parisian society without being immensely rich" (I.92). Painter provides complex reasons to explain the social eminence of Count Robert de Montesquiou, the model for the monstrous Baron de Charlus: it "was based partly on his snob-value as a titled intellectual, partly on his hypnotic power of imposing himself on the fashionable world, and partly on the gift his hated relatives possessed for intermarriage with the great" (I.125). Painter describes Montesquiou's manners, his Wildean wit ("It's bad enough not to have any money, it would be too much if one had to deprive oneself of anything," I.127), his behavior (he never realized his artistic potential but merely "dressed, collected, scribbled, quarrelled, fascinated and terrorised," I.133), and his sexual tastes (his carnal relations with the divine Sarah Bernhardt were followed by a week of uncontrollable vomiting). More importantly, Painter shows how their relations changed as Proust transformed Montesquiou in his fiction; how Proust's suffering in love unexpectedly revealed another side of his friend's peculiar personality and inspired a rare letter "of genuine, winning sympathy with which this saturnine man revealed, sometimes, the goodness that still lingered in his corroded heart" (II.206).

The appearance, conversation and character of Proust himself are also vividly delineated. Lucien Daudet remembered "his moonlike paleness and jet-black hair, his over-large head drooping on his narrow shoulders, and his enormous eyes, which seemed to take in everything at once without actually looking at anything" (I.186). Proust—who slept in the day, worked by night and found the sun "a very strange object"— would often converse with his friends till dawn, "growing ever more brilliant to stave off the moment of parting. . . . His conversation was full of the most piercing psychological observations, and anecdotes of gentle but penetrating irony" (I.257, 294). Claude Debussy, however, felt Proust was "longwinded and precious and a bit of an old woman" (I.291). Painter provides particularly interesting accounts of Proust's military service, when, among the discipline and love of comrades, he experienced the delightful illusion of being normal and accepted; of his duel, when he exchanged shots at twenty-five yards and showed considerable coolness and courage (he was also fearless of danger during wartime air-raids); and of his almost imperceptible sinecure as a librarian.

One of Painter's great strengths as a biographer is his ability to represent the complex motives of human behavior, to trace the recurrent patterns of Proust's life, and to delineate the major themes of the novel. He gives many reasons for Proust's courtship and flattery of Montesquiou—amiable, utilitarian, aesthetic, psychiatric—and concludes that Proust felt his own destiny as a man and a writer was linked to Count Robert. In a similar fashion, Painter explains that Proust did not object when his mother tried to find him a wife, "whether from desire to please her, or to conceal his perversion, or from confidence that he could always refuse any actual candidate for his hand, or because he had not yet entirely renounced the possibility of marriage" (I.247).

When tracing the dominant patterns of Proust's life, Painter notes that his "passion for Ruskin took precisely the same course as his love-affairs or ardent friendships. There was a prelude of tepid acquaintance; a crystallisation and a taking fire; and a falling out of love, from which he emerged free, but changed and permanently enriched" (I.256). He also observes that during Proust's ascent to the heights of the Faubourg Saint-Germain, he continued simultaneously his descent toward Sodom. And Painter concisely lists the major themes of *Remembrance of Things Past* as "the unreality of the phenomenal world, the poetic nature of the past in which the only true reality is hidden, the impossibility of knowing another person, the continual process of change in the self, feelings and memory" (I.69).

Painter told Grosskurth: "I went off Freud when I went off left-wing politics and the Popular Front before the war. . . . He was again and again presenting his theories as if he were scientifically proving them, and his texts contained no proof at all." Yet Painter qualified his "rejection" by adding, "Obviously there is a great deal of what Freud does say that is true" and by acknowledging, "Things like the Oedipus complex, love of one's mother and hostility against one's father, the encouragement of homosexuality by failure with [the] heterosexual love object, particularly when the family is involved in it, hostility between brothers, between children of the same parents—all of these I mention."[26]

Proust's doctor-father, who invented the principle of the *cordon sanitaire* and helped banish cholera from Europe, allowed his bewildering son to lead the life he wished. Proust's most profound and influential relationship was with his formidable and sacrificial mother. Painter observes early on that Proust "grew to believe, resentfully, that she loved him best when he was ill and he tried to win her love by being ill. . . . [Asthma] was the mark of his difference from others, his appeal for love, his refuge from duties which were foreign to his still unconscious purpose; and in later life it helped him to withdraw from the world and to produce a work 'de si longue haleine'. . . . Her blood made him a tribesman of Abraham, her over-anxious love a native of the Cities of the Plain" (I.4,12).[27]

Painter establishes that the loss and recovery of his mother's good-night kiss, described in the "Overture" to *Swann's Way*, was not an act of love but a surrender to his blackmail. Withheld at first by the command of his father and then indulgently bestowed, it symbolizes the nourishing but destructive adoration that prevented him from loving another woman and the mutual hatred "which persisted at the root of their love" (II.301). Proust consistently made heterosexual choices that were certain to fail, so that he would be free at last to choose his true desire. The mother's death, which marked the great watershed of Proust's life and is described at the beginning of the second volume, is poignantly rendered. After Proust had kissed his mother for the last time, he told a friend: "Today I have her still, dead, but accepting my caresses— tomorrow I shall lose her forever" (II.49).

One of Painter's principal points is that Proust's sexual experience, far from being exclusively homosexual, was partly based on his physical relations with women: "readers who have felt all along that Proust's picture of heterosexual love is valid and founded on personal experience will be glad to find their instinct justified" (I.xii). The female characters desired by the Narrator were not merely transposed from men, but began as women whom Proust was attracted to in real life: "In his novel Proust rejected his own inversion, and created the Narrator from the lost but real heterosexual part of his own divided nature; he used homosexuality, like snobbism and cruelty, as a symbol of universal original sin" (II.313).

Freud has taught modern biographers that it is essential to examine the sexual life of their subject, which was formerly considered either unknowable or unsuitable to know. By dealing with unpleasant truths and discussing Proust's perverse sexuality, Painter inevitably demythologizes (as the nineteenth-century biographers had idealized) the great writer; but he also brings us close to the inner man by providing the most sophisticated and complex view of Proust. A frank and full knowledge of Proust's homosexuality increases our understanding of the man and his novel, and enables us to participate in the transformation of life into art.

Painter's sensational disclosures about Proust's homosexual aberrations show that even the basest vices—the donation of his parents' furniture to a male brothel, the desecration of his mother's photograph, the indulgence in flagellation, the torture of rats with hatpins—were redeemed by his art. In a brilliant and discriminating summary that binds together the themes of Proust's life, Painter traces his vicious descent into the violence and cruelty of Sodom:

> [It] had begun with love for his equals (Reynaldo and Lucien), progressed through platonic affection for social superiors (Fénelon, Antoine Bibesco, and the rest) to physical affection for social inferiors (Ulrich and Agostinelli), and now ended, disillusioned with all, in a sterile intercourse with professional catamites. He was experimenting with evil—an evil which perhaps does not exist anywhere in the realm of natural or unnatural sex, except as a moral nullity, a mirage for the desperate—and testing his power to associate with it unscathed.

Painter emphasizes that one of the greatest novels ever written was created, paradoxically, from the basest material. Though he makes a moral judgment on these disheartening events, he also encourages compassion and forgiveness: though this vice "revealed itself in acts which are at once abominable and absurd, [it] should be absolved with awe and sympathy by all of his sinful fellow-humans" (II.266–267).

Proust began his novel in July 1909, installed the famous cork walls in his bedroom, and started the long process of expansion and enrichment of his prearranged plan which would continue until the day of his death. *Swann's Way*, rejected for publication by André Gide and praised by Henry James as the greatest French novel since *The Charterhouse of Parma*, was published in November 1913. *Within a Budding Grove* won the postwar Goncourt Prize for the intellectual non-combatant in 1919 and led to the Legion of Honor the following year. From then on Proust raced to complete his novel against the threat of death: " 'Death pursues me, Céleste,' he said, 'I shan't have time to finish my corrections' " (II.356). But when he reached the moribund condition of one of his characters, he hastened to add some notes on the death of Bergotte.

It may have been possible to cure Proust's asthma, but he unconsciously preferred his illness and did not want to be cured. It freed him for isolation and for work, "widening," as he said, "by cutting down the undergrowth of pointless friendships, the avenues that lead to my solitude" (II.330). He spent the two years between 1905 and 1907 almost entirely confined to bed, indulging his regimen of insomnia, fumigation and drugs. When he contracted pneumonia and died in November 1922, his masterpiece, though still imperfect, was complete.

In the midst of an acute analysis of the relation of Proust's *Contre Sainte-Beuve* to *Remembrance of Things Past*, one third of the way through the second volume, Painter suddenly, and more clearly than ever, expounds his exalted biographical credo:

> The biographer's task is to . . . discover, beneath the mask of the artist's every-day, objective life, the secret from which he extracted his work; show how, in the apparently sterile persons and places of that external life, he found the hidden, universal meanings which are the themes of his book; and reveal the drama of the contrast and interaction between his daily existence and his incommensurably deeper life as a creator. (II.126)

Painter's *Marcel Proust* triumphantly fulfills what he believes to be the author's highest purpose: to communicate "the state of vision in which the book was written, so that the writer's revelation becomes the reader's" (II.35).

CHAPTER SEVEN

Leon Edel's *Henry James*

EUGENE GOODHEART

The myth of the autonomy of the work of art persists, and as long as it persists literary biography remains a suspect genre. We tend to associate the myth with the advent of high modernism. In *A Portrait of the Artist*, Stephen Dedalus imagines the artist performing a disappearing act, either into the narrative or on to Mount Olympus. T. S. Eliot speaks of the necessary impersonality of art, that is, the necessary escape from personality and emotion into art. And in our day, that loose confederation of "post-structuralists," masters and mistresses of *écriture*, speak of "the death of the author."

I speak of a myth, because it is evident, even to its creators, that the author exists or at least existed and that he made his art from the materials of his own life: inner experiences, external events that he might have observed, read about, heard about. *A Portrait* itself is testimony to the presence of the author. Stephen's declaration of disappearance does not solve the problem of the artist's presence. And in the sometimes forgotten conclusion to Eliot's statement in which he asserts the impersonality of art, he says with a poignancy that becomes more intense in the light of what we have recently learned about his life: "only those who have personality or emotions know what it means to want to escape from these things".[1]

The truth that the myth reflects is that the art is not a mimesis of the life, if mimesis is understood as correspondence. The artist transforms his experiences, and since the principle or principles of transformation have eluded readers, critics and scholars, the autonomy of the work of art may be the only viable assumption. Which is not to say that the curiosity about lives disappears. We may continue to want to know as much as we can possibly know about the lives of poets, novelists and dramatists. Testimony to the appetite for such information can be found in the numerous outsized biographies of writers, major and minor. But our curiosity should not delude us into thinking that the artist's work is the subject of biography.

Is it necessary to adopt an either/or view? Perhaps we will never discover or agree upon the principles of transformation, that is, the nature of the creative process. Yet we may speculate about the relationship between the life and the work and simply allow for the kind of response or judgment that any text allows for. We may be persuaded or unconvinced, shocked into recognition or unengaged. The test of a literary biography need not implicate the genre as a whole, it need concern only the particular biography. Or perhaps, more accurately, each literary biography may define the genre in its own way, implicitly and discursively, and we may want to judge it in relation to its particular subject.

Leon Edel's *Henry James* should be particularly illuminating in this respect. The five-volume work has been hailed by many as the greatest of modern literary biographies. Edel himself has been titled the Master (of the genre), the title given to James himself in his "late period." And Edel has reflected more than any other literary biographer about the nature of his art. In 1959, he produced *Literary Biography*, a little book written in the course of his work on James.

In *Literary Biography*, Edel conceives of the relationship between author and biographer as one of antagonistic struggle. The artist attempts to hide his secrets and the biographer attempts to discover them. This "model" of antagonism is derived from James himself, who in a number of works ("The Real Thing," "The Aspern Papers") dramatized the author's dread of the invasive threat of the biographer. (James burnt the letters sent to him as one way of forestalling his future biographers.) And in his own biographical forays (e.g., his essay on George Sand), he reprimanded his subjects for excessively exposing their private lives to public view. (It is as if James' biographical exercises were polemics against biography, or at least against invasive biography, for James also said that biography was "one of the great observed adventures of mankind."[2]) For Edel, however, the secret is not or should not be of prurient interest. The biographer is not a prosecutor, who wishes to expose and humiliate his subject. He wants to construct a coherent truth about the life, and the "secrets" necessarily enter into that truth, and then he wishes to relate the living truth to the art.

Before questioning the status of the "secrets" the biographer seeks to discover, I want to address the three types of biography Edel distinguishes: the chronicle, the portrait and a third type (the one which he practices), the narrative–pictorial:

> The first and most common is the traditional documentary biography, an integrated work in which the biographer arranges the materials—Boswell did this—so as to allow the voice of the subject to be heard constantly (even when that voice is heard in converse with his own biographer, as in the case of Boswell). The second type of biography is the creation, in words, of something akin to the painter's portrait. Here the picture is somewhat more circumscribed; it is carefully sketched in, and a frame is placed around. The third type, which has been fashioned increasingly in our time, is one in which the materials are melted down and in which the biographer is present in the work as omniscient narrator. We are given largely, in such a work, the biographer's vision of his subject. The first type of biography might be said to be chronicle; the second pictorial; the third narrative–pictorial or novelistic.[3]

Edel's typology omits one significant type, the critical biography (of which Lionel Trilling's *Matthew Arnold* is a masterly instance). Indeed, it may have been possible for Edel to claim the category for his own work. In any case, what critical biography shares with "the third type" is the interpretive impulse that requires the biographer to be critic as well as scholar. (According to Edel, the literary biographer of the third type is the most comprehensive of readers.) But Edel wants to make an even greater claim for the third type. The "narrative–pictorial" is the novelistic, the kind of art that James and his disciple Percy Lubbock (in *The Craft of Fiction*) devoted their lives to defining and elaborating. Edel's *Henry James* wants to be read as a work of novelistic art. How do we assess its claims as art, and the degree of its success and/or failure?

But first we must characterize Edel's narrative. What story does Edel tell of the life and the art? It is, as I understand it, a story of paradoxes, and of paradoxes that are not explicitly confronted in the biography. The five volumes are the product of an extraordinary devotion to, an unsurpassed exercise in empathy[4] with, the life of the novelist. And yet there is, in a sense, so little life beyond the novels themselves. Edel cites Percy Lubbock's belief that in James' case "biography should abdicate in favor of autobiography,"[5] and autobiography in James' case (*A Small Boy and Others, Notes of a Son and Brother* and *The Middle Years*) is, like the novels of James' late manner, elaborate fictions of the life rather than mimetic representations of it.

All the so-called secrets have been volatilized, rarefied, mystified. Consider this description of the notorious Vastation, the obscure and unspeakable hurt that has driven critics and scholars to conjectures and speculations:

> Two things and more had come up—the biggest of which, and very wondrous as bearing on any circumstance of mine, as having a grain of weight to spare for it, was the breaking out of the War. The other, the infinitely small affair in comparison, was a passage of personal history the most entirely personal, but between which, as a private catastrophe or difficulty, bristling with embarrassments, and the great public convulsion that announced itself in bigger terms each day, I felt from the very first an association of the closest, yet withal, I fear, almost of the least clearly expressible. . . .
>
> One had the sense, I mean, of a huge comprehensive ache, and there were hours at which one could scarce have told whether it came most from one's own poor organism, still so young and so meant for better things, but which had suffered particular wrong, or from the enclosing social body, a body rent with a thousand wounds and that thus treated one to the honour of a sort of tragic fellowship. The twenty minutes had sufficed, at all events, to establish a relation—a relation to everything occurring round me not only for the next four years but for long afterward—that was at once extraordinarily intimate and quite awkwardly irrelevant. . . .
>
> Jammed into the acute angle between two high fences, where the rhythmic play of my arms, in tune with that of several other pairs, but at a dire disadvantage of position, induced a rural, a rusty, a quasi-extemporised old engine to

work and a saving stream to flow, I had done myself, in face of a shabby conflagration, a horrid even if an obscure hurt; and what was interesting from the first was my not doubting in the least its duration—though what seemed equally clear was that I needn't as a matter of course adopt and appropriate it, so to speak, or place it for increase of interest on exhibition.[6]

Is it simply back-trouble, or an impotence-making injury, and what relation does it have to the Civil War? And what do we make of the proportionality of events to each other? We will never know, we are not intended to know.

James admitted that *Notes of a Son and Brother* (the second of the three autobiographies) was a re-creation of the life: "I did instinctively regard it last as all my truth, to do what I would with it."[7] Here James was simply asserting what he had learned in his practice as a novelist, that the "truth" of the past was available only through the refractions of creative memory. No less than in his novels, James felt no obligation to recover the past as it had been experienced in the past. His recovery of the past was intended to serve artistic "truth." Writing apropos of "The Turn of the Screw," Edel remarks that "like most artists [James] did not like to 'explain' his art, and he was determined not to spoil the mystification he had created."[8]

Edel, the necessary antagonist as biographer, seeks the secrets that the novelist desires to conceal. At the same time, given Edel's empathetic imagination, he resists the impulse to demystify. On the contrary, he wants to preserve the mystification. Indeed, the life would disappear in the demystification. In "melting down" the materials, Edel avoids the temptation (a temptation perhaps for another biographer, not for Edel) to find the dirty little secret. ("Physical habits of the creative personality, his 'sex life' or his bowel movements, belong to the 'functioning' being and do not reliably distinguish him from his fellow humans."[9]) Edel in effect finds a middle ground which enables him to uncover "the secrets" and to preserve a virtually empathetic sympathy with his subject—or at least, this would seem to be his intention.

What are the "secrets"? The first volume, *The Untried Years*, attempts to show in the life the origins of the artist and the kind of artist that James would become. The physically passive

James would become an actor, indeed a conqueror in art. Balzac, a counterpart of Napoleon in literature, would become James' model.[10] Implied, though not developed, is a theory of psychological compensation, a virtually Adlerian notion of physical puniness breeding grandiose ambitions. James' sense of his own personal weakness or vulnerability was, according to Edel, intensified by a sentiment of secondariness. He was the second son, brother to the older, impulsive, brilliant, expressive William. Edel finds the sentiment of secondariness displaced in the fiction to a "predilection for second sons" and the cultivation of "an ideal fatherless and brotherless state."[11] It would seem that Henry resolved his sibling rivalry with his brother by expatriating and becoming homeless.

Has Edel discovered a secret? "Secret," I think, is a deceptive term because it implies the conscious withholding of an event or thing by the subject, the revelation of which might alter in a significant way our understanding of the subject. "Secret" is deceptive in its implication of deception: we are not to trust, for instance, the surface imagination of the subject either in his artistic works or his letters, because he tries to conceal an opposite or radically different truth. Certainly James did not consciously withhold any truth that Edel believes to be significant. He did not think of himself as engaged in a fierce Oedipal rivalry with his brother. He may have thought himself inferior to his brother on more than one occasion but the sense of inferiority, though colored by envy or regret, did not affect his deep conscious affection and admiration of his brother. If there is a "secret," it is of the unconscious kind, a secret from James himself. But then secret may be the wrong word, for it displaces to the objective realm what is after all a function of biographical interpretation. "Oedipal rivalry" is a psychoanalytic construction of Edel's, belonging to the arena of contending interpretations about the reality of James' consciousness.

In asserting this view, I am not capitulating to the theoretical claims of reader-centered critics who tend to deny the objective reality of texts. On the contrary, I am contrasting the objective evidence of texts, for instance, James' avowed affection for his brother, with the interpretations that gainsay or qualify the evidence. Nor am I even saying that the evidence proves the interpretation wrong. Such a view allows too much authority to surface evidence, the kind of authority that would make interpretation supererogatory. But the distinction is essential to preserve the very contention of interpretations that makes interpretation a vital activity. Edel's omniscient way with the evidence (his exclusion of other interpretive voices from the narrative) proceeds from the hubristic, if not false, presumption that he has recovered all the secrets and that he is in full possession of the truth. It is no argument in his behalf that he has mastered all the archives as no one else has and that he has presented his view of the life in five massive volumes. Indeed, for all of Edel's unquestioned mastery of the James materials (the remaining archives of his letters were enormous and fully possessed by Edel while he was writing the biography), there is relatively little evidence of the workings of scholarship in the exposition. This most scholarly of biographies makes the most unscholarly impression. Edel's narrative has the deliberate seamlessness of a novel with abundant episodes. There are relatively few foregrounded cruxes for interpretation. Edel does not argue or debate, he tells a story. Perhaps he feels he does not have to argue or debate, because he is in full possession of the evidence. No amount of evidence can guarantee the truth of an interpretation, since it is always based on one of a number of possible shapings of the evidence. One may even fault Edel's strategy of massive construction by arguing that it masks the interpretive character of his enterprise.

What should we make of Edel's psychoanalytic bias? Perhaps the first thing to note is its simplicity. In an essay "The Figure Under the Carpet,"[12] Edel argues for the duality of the self, in which the manifest content is in conflict with the latent content. The biographer is not content merely to trace the figure *in* the carpet, he wants to know the figure *under* the carpet as well. The figure under the carpet is, of course, inference rather than fact. As I have already suggested, it is a function of a psychological theory that suspects the given, that sees the given in terms of its opposite: the given, the surface, is concealment or compensation, but it is never coincident with the figure *under the carpet*. Edel discovers the figure of sibling rivalry under the apparent affection between the brothers. He also finds underneath the admiration Henry expressed for the extraordinary women in his life (his mother, his sister Alice, Minny Temple, his fictional creations, Isabel Archer, Milly Theale) a deep unconscious fear of women as threatening witches. In Edel's reading, this fear registers in the sense of terror in a number of James' tales. Note the figure under the carpet is common to both the life and the art.

Edel's psychoanalytic reading of James' life seems to be independent of his scholarship. It is not as if Edel has evidence of a figure under the carpet from the life, which he can then show to be concealed in the art. The underlying figure is supposed to be common to both the art and the life and both the figure and its transformations are the constructions of the biographer. Edel's authority as a scholar emboldens him to a certain freedom from scholarship as in his interpretation of James' notorious notation: "Ledward—Bedward—Dedward—Deadward." For Edel, James' note implies an association between death and marriage.

The psychoanalytic interpretation, while not all-consuming, is an intrinsic part of Edel's story and resistible only if one makes demands on Edel that one makes on a scholar. Edel's narrative strategy is to disarm the reader and avoid the demands. (It is incidentally a curious fact about Edel's approach that his psychoanalytic interest in James goes along with an almost Victorian reticence about the facts that normally count in psychoanalytic interpretation: "the physical habits . . . 'sex life,' " etc. It is very much an antiseptic psychoanalysis. In remarking this fact, I am not necessarily endorsing a more vigorous, less reticent psychoanalytic approach. What I do feel is the lack of conviction and persuasiveness in what may simply pass, in the eyes of other readers, as tact.)

Having expressed these rather severe reservations about Edel's method, I continue to find his intuitions about the life impressive and provocative, even when not entirely persuasive, and the story extremely compelling. *The Untried Years*, however one may dissent from Edel's judgments, is an extraordinary biographical achievement. The melting down of materials and their transformation produce narrative persuasiveness that one almost never encounters in biography. There are, to be sure, already symptoms, anticipations of the dangers of supersaturation to which Edel is committed. The epigraph to the second volume, *The Conquest of London*, is a quotation from James: "The great thing is to be *saturated* with something." *Henry James* is a biography of saturation. Edel never produces a laundry list, so to speak, the vice of so many "monumental biographies," but there is an almost deliberate retardation of narrative movement, a marking time, which seems to have as its aim a mimesis of the life as actually lived: an inconsequence of days, of dinners, of letter writing. James himself anticipated this judgment. Writing to Henry Adams about his biography of William Wetmore Story, an American lawyer and would-be artist, James notes that "the truth [is that] any retraced story of bourgeois lives (lives other than great lives of 'action'—et encore!) throws a chill upon the scene . . . the art of the biographer—devilish art!—is somehow practically thinning."[13] The life is composed of observation, not action, and Edel wishes to reflect both the density and expansiveness of the *activity* of observation, but the effect is "practically thinning."

Quentin Anderson, a severe though not wholly unsympathetic critic of the biography, praises Edel for his success in "secur[ing] a sense of the passage of time," but, as Anderson also notes, Edel's "retrospective" technique in each of the 250 or so titled sections tends toward "a miniature completeness of statement," a self-sufficient lucidity that makes for "leveled diction" and the lack of "detailed argument."[14] One might add that the technique may falsify the way time passes by suggesting that every event in James' life contributed to a teleological fulfillment.

But it may not be so much the passage of time that Edel is after as the explanation of events. Consider Edel's defense of Leonard Woolf's anti-chronological method of accounting for Virginia's breakdown in a review of another biography which follows the chronological method:

> Had [Woolf] followed Kendall's prescription, he would have given us a step-by-step account of Virginia Woolf's nervous breakdowns in 1913, 1915, the 1920's, the late 1930's, each pigeon-holed in their proper year. Instead, when he reaches her first breakdown in 1913 he relates her entire medical history, moving forward and backward in time between 1913 and 1941. There is no question that we are thus made to grasp the full heroism of Mrs. Woolf's struggle against the insanity that constantly threatened to engulf her creativity. The impact would have been greatly diluted had we been given the illnesses in their scattered chronological moments among the other events and personages of her life.[15]

The carefully shaped vignette with its combining and counterpointing of events, past and present, compensates for the sense of thinness. The price that Edel pays is an almost melodramatic repetitiousness in the representation of the life.

Anderson also notes that the sense of time in the biography is insulated from political and social time, "Gladstone or that of the Paris Commune, or to take figures closer to home, that of the public salience of the elder James or William James."[16] But this lack, contributing to a sense of thinness, may be a function of the insular character of James' life.

The main subject or "action" of the second volume is the Englishing of James, who apparently did not take to England or London immediately. We know that England's imaginative importance for James became in part its "codes and rules, and its stratified class structure [which] provided Henry with a standard for cross cultural judgments."[17] But the interest of the second volume is not in the resultant knowledge. Rather it is in the representation of the *experience* of London, and in the personal dramas that played themselves out in James' imagination, if not in his life—if one can sustain such a distinction. The main drama concerns Constance Fenimore Woolson, a niece of James Fenimore Cooper, and it implicates the question of James' problematic, fascinated and fascinating relationship to women. If Fenimore Woolson loved James, as one must conclude from Edel's account, the natures and circumstances of both Fenimore (as she is called) and Henry conspire to refract, deflect, divert, to do everything but make the consummation possible. Edel sees Fenimore in the figure of May Bartram (in "The Beast in the Jungle"), and Edel's rendering of the relationship suggests the imaginative abortiveness of the relationship in the great short novel.

Fenimore, it would seem, played a major role in James' life, because she brought to the surface, as no other woman had, his passional or erotic incapacity. Her suicide shattered him in the way May Bartram's death "annihilated" John Marcher. The beast had sprung, and his response would be the dramatization of the central predicament of his life, the dramatization itself being part of the predicament. Millicent Bell points out that the theme of "the woman who offers love to a man who fails to appreciate the gift" is present in James' writings before Miss Woolson's death.[18] One might argue that her death intensified his imaginative sense of the situation. As Edel puts it, "Henry's tales of the artist-life invariably contain the admonition that marriage could only be a burden to the creator, a distraction, a form of servitude fatal to art."[19]

At the same time James shows the inordinate price paid for the art—an impoverishment of life, on which James' art placed a supreme value. What mutes the predicament is that James "succeeded" (as his great contemporary and friend, Flaubert, did not) in assimilating the energies of life to art itself. James' art is not made from impoverishment, but rather from the displacement of those erotic and passional energies from the life to the art. James himself had expressed the relationship between art and life in a paradoxical manner. "I live, live intensely and am fed by life, and my value, whatever it be, is my own kind of expression that Art *makes* life, makes interest, makes importance."[20] Fed by life, art makes life. This is the paradox that lies at the heart of Strether's affirmation in *The Ambassadors*.

In a critical essay on Edel's biography, Mark Krupnick speaks of James' "increasing insistence on the all-sufficiency of consciousness and the omnipotence of the artist" as a denial of the feeling "that he had missed out on life. It was art that made life."[21] And he sees Edel himself as complicit in the Jamesian rationalization: "Professor Edel's biography is an American romance, in which the scholar has merged himself with the artist and taken on his omnipotence."[22] Unlike other critics of Edel, who take him to task for psychoanalytic inventions for which they see little evidence, Krupnick stresses Edel's defensiveness against a true, though subversive, understanding of James' imperial fantasies about the artist and his deeds. He cites, for example, Edel's resistance to Dr. Joseph Collins' diagnosis of James in 1911 during a period of chronic depression.

Collins wrote that James had "an enormous amalgam of the feminine in his makeup; he displayed many of the characteristics of adult infantilism; he had a singular capacity for detachment from reality and with it a dependence upon realities that was even pathetic. He had a dread of ugliness in all forms. . . . His amatory coefficient was comparatively low; his gonadal sweep was too narrow."[23] Krupnick concedes the jargon of the last sentence, but he contends that "Collins's account is far more perceptive on the psychological side than Edel's 2000 pages." Whatever the relative merits of Edel's and Collins' psychologies, it is difficult to see how the language of Collins' understanding would have illuminated James' writing. It is not merely a question of a lapse into jargon; it is rather a matter of finding a psychological language appropriate to the imaginative idiom of the subject. Complicity of the kind Edel exhibits may obliterate a necessary critical distance, but it is the understandable consequence of a desire to enter the subject's consciousness empathically.

The essential issue here is the art–life opposition, which James sought to overcome in imagination or consciousness. For Krupnick, the Jamesian commitment to art is sheer rationalization (Flaubert's hatred of life would be the honest consequence of an overweening artistic devotion). I think the judgment of denial or repression or rationalization is too facile in James' case. It dismisses the energies and excitements of consciousness to which James attached the word "life"—or refuses to credit them. James *lived* through his mind in an unusual and impressive way. His way may not provide a model for others, but to deny this fact is to deny a life-possibility.

This peculiarly Jamesian "solution" is, I think, the justification for the "mystification" and for the impertinence of any demystifying criticism or biography. The "truth" of James or of any of his incapable heroes does not lie in their incapacity (or, at least, that is not the interesting—a favorite Jamesian word— truth). It lies rather in the transformations of the failed energy into art, that is into image, similitude, narrative sentence. Long after we make the discovery (in "The Beast in the Jungle") of Marcher's incapacity, a plain fact or truth, uninteresting in itself, the extraordinary images that fill the void that the fiction represents reverberate in our imaginations with an infinite suggestiveness:

> Her face and her voice, all at his service now, worked the miracle—the impression operating like the torch of a lamplighter who touches into flame, one by one, a long row of gas-jets.✳
>
> They were literally afloat together; for our gentleman this was quite marked, quite as marked as that the fortunate cause of it was just the buried treasure of her knowledge. He has with his own hands dug up this little hoard, brought to

✳ *These paragraphs are not consecutive in the story.*

light—that is to within reach of the dim day constituted by their discretions and privacies—the object of value the hiding place of which he had, after putting it into the ground himself so strangely, so long forgotten.

Perhaps nowhere did James express the sense of the barrenness of his life more poignantly than in a letter that he wrote to his American journalist friend in Paris, Morton Fullerton: "The port from which I set out was, I think, that of the essential loneliness of my life—and it seems to be the port also, in sooth, to which my course finally directs itself! This loneliness . . . what is it still but the deepest thing about one? Deeper, about me, at any rate, than anything else; deeper than my 'genius,' deeper than my 'discipline,' deeper than my pride, deeper, above all, than the deep counterminings of art."[24] Loneliness can be found in the most intense activity, the most extraordinary eventfulness. One has the impression from the life and from the insistent "deeper" in James' letter that James had plumbed the depths in the uneventfulness of his external life. What the letter fails to honor sufficiently in the imbalance created by the repetition of "deeper" are the "counterminings" of the art. The events of James' life were, essentially, the profusion of works that dramatized the rich and continuous activity of consciousness. James was the least aphoristic of artists, for aphorisms in their economy and closure would have opened up the abysses of loneliness and emptiness that must have always threatened him.

If this is so, then it may be a misrepresentation of the "case" to speak of the biographical element as concealed, as Edel does. Edel characterizes the famous preoccupation with point of view as an exercise in concealment. "James sought to cover up what he was doing . . . by using shifting angles of vision so as to make us feel the way in which people see one another."[25] But this multiplicity of vision is where the truth lies, not in some single positivist fact of "what he was doing." Point of view does not necessarily imply concealment. Rather it suggests the partial accessibility to truth of every finite mind. Edel's narrative is controlled by the "omniscient" perspective that James rejected for his own fiction. The interest of a Jamesian story is in the inextinguishable sense of complexity or mystery in the presented character. And the complexity or mystery demands a continuous awareness of the problematics of perspective. Edel's narrative effortlessly effaces "the point of view," the effect of which is a transparency of representation at odds with the baroque mystifications of the prose. If Edel had paid more attention to James' prose (where the aesthetic mystifications are generated), his story would not have been so effortlessly authoritative.

What then is the role of biography in interpretation or explanation? By tactfully juxtaposing the life to the art, Edel "uncovers," so to speak, the narrative patterns of James' consciousness, patterns that he lived as well as transformed into art. They are, for the most part, patterns of consciousness, close to the visible impressions of the art (e.g., the James–Woolson relationship requires little translation or transformation into the Marcher–May Bartram relation), not hidden latent structures that are transformed into the art (though Edel's conception of a sibling rivalry between Henry and William may qualify as such).

The Wings of the Dove, a novel of James' late period, offers us an opportunity of examining Edel's manner of showing how James turned his life into art. (Edel's discussion of *The Wings of the Dove* occurs in the final volume.) Edel attributes its origin to the early death of his gifted and beloved cousin Minny Temple in 1870, thirty-one years before he had begun dictating the novel. The association of names (Minny Temple and Milly Theale) is clear enough. Edel sees the novel as a culmination of a long mourning, but also as a "welcome" opportunity for totally possessing her in his mind and memory. In contrasting his own emergence from ill-health during the time of the Civil War and her "sinking out of brightness and youth into decline and death" (in James' words), James "made it sound as if she had laid down her life that he might live."[26] (This is a characteristic Edelian novelistic leap beyond the evidence.) Edel adduces other little known works by James ("De Grey: A Romance," "Long-Staff's Marriage" and "Georgina's Reason," in which two women bear names similar to those in *Wings*, Kate and Mildred Theory) to elicit what he believes to be the determining fantasy of all these fictions, the displacement of love from the living to the dead as substitute for another Jamesian theme, the renunciation of marriage. (Does this mean that Minny Temple's salvational dying consisted in freeing James from the threat of loving and marrying Minny?)

Edel brings in a complex of other material, the death of

Constance Fenimore Woolson in 1894, the curious relationship of his need for and his devotion to a "sacred woman" who served his spiritual needs, but who also threatened him with physical demands which had to be renounced. "The myth of the ethereal and the fleshly, of spirit and body continued to have reality. Otherwise stated, in James' equations, they were formulated as art and passion—and in his existence they could not be reconciled. The solution: renunciation. One renounced love, or was deprived of it. Accepted, it could prove ruinous."[27] But the renunciation is not as stable as the "equations" imply. James writes *The Wings of the Dove* at a time when, according to Edel, he had opened himself up to the meaning of physical love in his relationship with the sculptor Hendrik Anderson. The renunciation, it would seem, is threatened, though Edel does not quite say this.

Edel's exposition of the psychological impulsions of the novel appears to lose its track in speculation about James' double relationship to the "literal realism of Balzac" and symbolism or the "evocative realism of Ibsen."[28] But in briefly exploring its symbolic aspect, in particular the scriptural source of the title, Edel discovers a flaw "within the inventive poetry and form of *The Wings of the Dove*": Merton Densher, the apparently "active and even coercive lover," is "in reality the classical passive, renunciatory Jamesian hero."[29] The dead Milly commands his devotion as the live one never did, and Kate, the "villainous" fleshly heroine must be renounced. Edel continues his discussion of the novel with a formal analysis which points out its "strange organization." "The great scenes—all the expected ones— [between Milly and Densher] are left out." (James himself spoke of the *Wings* as suffering from a "misplaced pivot: . . . as having too big a head for its body."[30]) And he concludes with a speculation that the model for Merton Densher was his journalist friend W. Morton Fullerton, who, it turns out, was like James himself in "his own reticences, his problems in relating to women."[31]

Edel's dense, largely speculative adducing of biographical material to his reading of the novel gives it an orchestration, so to speak, that one does not find in a strictly interpretive reading, but it does not change or extend or deepen an interpretation one might make without the biographical knowledge. The effect is textural rather than cognitive.

Since there is so little external event in James' life, the
"progress" of the biography must be measured by the progress
of James' consciousness. The third volume, *The Middle Years*
(1882–1895), shows James at the end of his "international
tales." The image of the portraitist, already strongly anticipated
in the earlier volumes, is confirmed. Edel provides a fine
extended comparison between James and John Singer Sargent,
his friend and painter of James' portrait. As Edel notes, both
James and Sargent were portraitists of great ladies. If Edel were
writing cultural history as well as biography, he might have
speculated about the abundance of portraits of "great" ladies in
nineteenth-century literature (Emma Bovary, Dorothea Brooke,
Anna Karenina, Catherine Earnshaw), the "heroization" of
love, the "feminine" emotion. The cultural dimension is missing
in Edel's work.

James' famous interest in the scenic, with its origins in the
painterly, had been earlier "documented" by Edel in his
description of James' walks in New York, in which he was
continually taking in the scene. But the distinction of the
Jamesian portrait is not in the external notation of the
physiognomy of the subject, but in its psychological and moral
lineaments. (The contrast is made in this respect between
James and Maupassant.) Portraits appear everywhere in James,
in *The Bostonians*, an essentially failed novel in Edel's view, in *The
Portrait of a Lady* and in his story "The Liar." James, an
inveterate traveler, even characterizes "Florence . . . as beautiful,
and somehow as personal—and as talkative—as a lovely
woman."[32] One of Edel's considerable achievements is to present
the erotics of landscape in James' imagination. *The Middle Years*
is itself a portrait of an artist who has achieved authority. One
cannot make the criticism of James that James made of his
friend, the novelist Vernon Lee: she had committed "the
unpardonable sin," and "had taken a portrait from life" and
"had not exposed it to the process of art."[33] The sin was against
both life and art. James did not forgive violations of privacy,
betrayals of the secrets of friendship; nor did he value an art
that was incapable of imaginatively transforming the facts of
life. One almost has the feeling from both the autobiography
and the biography that all of life sat, as it were, for a portrait.

And yet, no biographer or critic can simply remain content
with the artistic transformation, the mystification. In Volume

IV, *The Treacherous Years*, and again in Volume V, *The Master*, Edel addresses as delicately as possible the question of James' sexual personality. James' relationship to the sculptor Hendrik Anderson was probably not overtly homosexual. It was marked by the evasiveness and suggestiveness of James' relationship with women, in particular with Fenimore—and which we find dramatized in so many of James' fictions. But Edel discovers an intensity of feeling in James' relations with Anderson that suggests a homosexual bias. "In opening himself to feeling in recent months, in allowing himself to experience the touch, the presence, the embrace, of the young sculptor, James had learned the meaning of love."[34] Here we have Edel, the novelist, extending, if not inventing the facts, beyond what the documents provide. Edel's characterization, however, in the Jamesian spirit, remains discreet. He never speaks of James as a homosexual. If anything, Edel makes us feel the powerful resistance (overcoming temptation) to sexual practice. Indeed, he defends James against what he considers Hugh Walpole's scurrilous story that he had offered himself to the Master and the Master had said "I can't, I can't."[35] Edel's dismissal of Walpole's story is based on an "argument" so devious and obscure that one cannot make head or tail of it. It is a case— and not the only one in the biography—of special pleading that proceeds from an empathy with his subject.

James' relationship to Hendrik Anderson has an interest beyond the question of James' sexuality. It involves James' conception of art, a conception to which the vainglories of Anderson's art would prove to be a foil. Anderson was a sculptor with monumental ambitions, who tried in a single stroke, so to speak, to create a world, the kind of artist that "could adorn great Mussolini manifestations of public frenzy and national megalomania."[36] James too was a world-maker: consider only his desire to emulate Balzac, a Napoleon among novelists. And yet James fully understood and practiced the humilities that make great art. In a letter to Anderson, James chastizes Anderson's megalomaniacal utopianism, speaking of "thing[s] struggl[ing] into life, even the very best of them, by slow steps and stages and rages and convulsions of experience, and utterly refus[ing] to be taken over ready-made or *en bloc*."[37] The difference between James and Anderson was, of course, a difference between genius and mediocrity, but it is also a difference in aesthetic ideology (a word James would have detested), expressive of the difference between genius and mediocrity.

I leave for last, or next to last, a question that is often foremost in discussions of the biography. Is the extraordinary length of the biography justified? Edel has recently condensed with some revision the five volumes into one volume, presumably to invite a larger readership. He has also, so he claims, brought the work up to date, adding new material and revising its language somewhat, but the claim for its status as masterpiece depends upon its multi-volumed version—in its strength and its vulnerability. So the question persists. Is this life or any life for that matter worth five volumes? My own answer is determined by the character of the life, its intersection with the larger political, social and spiritual forces of the age. Joseph Frank's projected five-volume critical biography of Dostoyevsky may be justified in part by the novelist's extraordinary involvement with the political and religious history of his time—so the volumes are exercises in political and religious history as well as in biography and criticism. But James' life is another matter. As one reads Edel, one is continually impressed by James' relative innocence of the momentous political events he might have experienced. The Civil War is a presence, but the Vastation, the obscure psychological and physiological disaster he experienced, looms much larger in his imaginative life. Even as "recorder" of social life, James' world seems so rarefied, so invented that it is not always clear what its sources in actual social experience is. My answer then is that the five volumes are not justified, that "the thinning out" that James complained about in biography is in great part a function of this particular life, the life of Henry James.

What then remains of the claim for Edel's work as a masterpiece? Edel has remained true to the extraordinary disproportion between the life and the art—that is, between the thinness of the life and the richness of the art. Whatever we may think of Edel's particular interpretations of the works of art, of the life into the art, the biography remains an extraordinary tribute to the "writer's writings," as Quentin Anderson puts it. If it succeeds, it is in its capacity to represent the narrative fantasies that grew out of the life. The contention that Edel has invented or misrepresented those fantasies is a most damaging criticism. I do not share the view that Edel is a misrepresenter or a fabricator, though alternative interpretations are always possible. What the biography clearly fails to do is to "imitate," so to speak, the complex syntax of James' imagination. The very length of the biography creates the expectation and makes its disappointment all the more serious.

I should say in conclusion that I can think of no other work that provokes in the critical reader so many strictures, reservations and fundamental objections as does Edel's *Henry James* and yet manages to triumph over them and tell an engrossing story.

Notes

Introduction: *Jeffrey Meyers*

1. Leon Edel, *Writing Lives: Principia Biographica* (New York, 1984), p. 30.
2. Phyllis Grosskurth, "An Interview with George Painter," *Salmagundi*, 6 (1983), 37.
3. Lord St. Leonards, *Misrepresentations in Campbell's Lives of Lyndhurst and Brougham* (London, 1869), p. 3.
4. *The Autobiography of Henry Taylor* (London, 1885), II.193.
5. Quoted in Edel, *Writing Lives*, pp. 116–117.
6. Henry James, "George Sand," *Selected Literary Criticism*, ed. Morris Shapira (London, 1963), p. 160.
7. Henry Adams, *Letters (1892–1918)*, ed. Worthington Ford (Boston, 1938), p. 495.
8. Lord Birkenhead, *Rudyard Kipling* (London, 1978), p. 343.
9. Rudyard Kipling, "The Appeal," *Kipling's Verse* (Garden City, New York, 1942), p. 836.
10. Roy Campbell, *Wyndham Lewis*, ed. Jeffrey Meyers (Pietermaritzburg: University of Natal Press, 1985), pp. 6, 10.
11. Vladimir Nabokov, *The Real Life of Sebastian Knight* (Norfolk, Conn., 1941), p. 15.
12. Vladimir Nabokov, *Look at the Harlequins!* (London, 1975), p. 226.
13. Philip Larkin, "Posterity," *High Windows* (New York, 1974), p. 27. In October 1986 J. D. Salinger, a reclusive author with a strong sense of privacy, prevented the publication of Ian Hamilton's biography, which had been printed and even reviewed (in the *New Criterion*), but not yet sold in bookstores.
14. Ralph Waldo Emerson, "History," *Essays* (Boston, 1925), p. 10.

15. W. B. Yeats, "Introduction to *The Resurrection*," *Explorations* (London, 1962), p. 397.

16. T. S. Eliot, "The Function of Criticism," *On Poetry and Poets* (New York, 1957), p. 123.

17. W. H. Auden, "Who's Who," *Collected Poems*, ed. Edward Mendelson (London, 1976), p. 109. In "The Six Napoleons," *The Return of Sherlock Holmes* (London, 1970), p. 183, Arthur Conan Doyle—like the literary biographer—connects fact and detection: " 'Well, Mr. Holmes, what are we to do with that fact?' 'To remember it—to docket it. We may come on something later which will bear upon it.' " See also David Irving's "Author's Foreword" to *The War Path: Hitler's Germany, 1933–1939* (New York, 1978), p. 6: historical research means "intuitively registering egregious facts in the hope that some of them may, perhaps, click with facts found years later in another file five thousand miles away."

18. Edmund Clerihew Bentley, *Biography for Beginners* (London, 1905), n.p., slightly misquoted in W. H. Auden and Louis MacNeice, *Letters From Iceland* (London, 1937), p. 214.

19. Stephen Spender, *Journals, 1939–1983*, ed. John Goldsmith (New York, 1986), p. 158.

20. See Donald Greene, " 'Tis a Pretty Book, Mr. Boswell, But—," *Georgia Review*, 32 (Spring 1978), 18–20.

21. Leon Edel, "The Art of Biography," *Paris Review*, 98 (Winter 1985), 171, 187.

22. Edel, *Writing Lives*, p. 31. In addition to Leon Edel, the most recent books on biography are: James Veninga, ed., *The Biographer's Gift: Life Histories and Humanism* (College Station, Texas, 1983); William Empson, *Using Biography* (Cambridge, Mass., 1984); Ira Nadel, *Biography: Fiction, Fact and Form* (London, 1984); Milton Lomask, *The Biographer's Craft* (New York, 1986); William Zinsser, ed., *Extraordinary Lives: The Art and Craft of American Biography* (New York, 1986); Stephen Oates, ed., *Biography as High Adventure* (Amherst, Mass., 1986); Ruth Hoberman, *Modernizing Lives* (Carbondale, Illinois, 1986).

23. This book, which offers extended analyses of representative works, could also have included Lockhart's *Scott*, Gaskell's *Brontë*, Froude's *Carlyle*, Deutscher's *Trotsky*, Jones' *Freud*, Erikson's *Luther* and Marchand's *Byron*.

24. Strachey's influence can be seen in modern fiction as well

as biography, most recently in the mannered style, witty remarks and contemptuous attitude of Giles Fox (who shares Strachey's first name and guile), the hero of A. N. Wilson's *Wise Virgin* (1982).

1 Johnson's *Life of Savage*: Donald Greene

1. Samuel Johnson, *Early Biographical Writings*, ed. J. D. Fleeman (Farnborough, Hants., 1973). The biographies of physicians in Robert James' *Medical Dictionary*, however, have recently been argued not to be by Johnson.
2. An excellent analysis of the *Life of Drake* by O. M. Brack, Jr., is scheduled to appear in *The Task of an Author: Essays on Samuel Johnson's Achievement*, ed. Prem Nath (Troy, New York, forthcoming).
3. Peter Millard, in his edition of Roger North's *General Preface and Life of Dr. John North* (Toronto, 1984), p. 15. Excerpts from the *General Preface* were earlier published by James L. Clifford in his *Biography as an Art* (New York, 1962).
4. Samuel Johnson, *Letters*, ed. R. W. Chapman (Oxford, 1952), Letter No. 729.2 (May 1781).
5. G. B. Hill in his edition of *The Lives of the English Poets* (even he omits "and a criticism on their works") (Oxford, 1905) conveniently numbers the paragraphs of each, facilitating calculations of length. From these I have sometimes omitted material that is not strictly part of the preface, such as the reprinted essay on Pope's epitaphs.
6. Including good stories that have now been discredited, such as that about Dryden's saying "Cousin Swift, you will never be a poet."
7. The last sentence comes from the companion essay, *Idler* 84, on autobiography.
8. Preface to *Eminent Victorians* (1918).
9. See note 3 above.
10. Clarence Tracy, *The Artificial Bastard: A Biography of Richard Savage* (Cambridge, Mass., 1953), pp. 5–6. In the account that follows, I rely heavily on Tracy.
11. Such actions were not uncommon in the history of the British peerage. See G. E. C., *The Complete Peerage*, I.367, notes a and b, where seven cases are cited in which the

legal doctrine "Pater est quem nuptiae demonstrant" was overruled by the House of Lords, and a son born to the wife of a peer was denied succession to her husband's peerage.

12. Tracy, *The Artificial Bastard*, p. 27.
13. Hawkins, *Life of Samuel Johnson*, ed. Bertram Davis (New York, 1961), p. 29.
14. The most devout modern believer in "Savage" is Anthony West, the illegitimate son of Rebecca West and H. G. Wells. In his novel *Heritage*, 1953, he named the protagonist, the illegitimate son of a famous woman who is indifferent to him, "Richard Savage." Shortly after Dame Rebecca's death, West published an article, "Mother and Son" (*New York Review of Books*, March 1, 1984), in which he states that his "Savage" was autobiographical, and violently attacked his mother's memory, comparing her to Lady Macclesfield. When I pointed out that there was no hard evidence that Johnson's "Savage" was Lady Macclesfield's son, West was outraged (*NYRB*, June 14). How could a modern academic think he knew as much about the matter as Johnson? "Johnson was *there!*" But of course, at the crucial times, Johnson was no more "there" than I was.
15. Edmund Bergler, "Samuel Johnson's Life of the Poet Richard Savage—A Paradigm for a Type," *American Imago*, 4 (1947), 42–64.
16. Hawkins, *Life of Samuel Johnson*, p. 29.
17. James Boswell, *Life of Johnson*, ed. G. B. Hill, rev. L. F. Powell (Oxford, 1934), III.51.
18. Tracy, *The Artificial Bastard*, p. 4.
19. Waugh, *Put Out More Flags* (London, 1942), p. 58. Basil is the central character of this and another early novel, *Black Mischief*, 1932. In the last piece of fiction Waugh wrote before his death, *Basil Seal Rides Again*, 1963, Basil is revived and up to his old tricks.
20. Johnson, *An Account of the Life of Savage*, ed. Clarence Tracy (Oxford, 1971), p. 60. Cited below as *Account*.
21. Diderot, *Oeuvres complètes* (Paris, 1875), IX.451:

C'est une étrange femme que cette comtesse de Manlesfield [*sic*], qui poursuit un enfant de l'amour avec une rage qui se soutient pendant de longues années, qui ne s'éteint jamais, et qui n'est fondée sur rien. Si un poëte s'avisait d'introduire, dans un drame ou dans un roman, un caractère de cette espèce, il serait sifflé; il est cependant dans la nature. On siffle donc quelquefois la nature? Et pourquoi non? Ne le mérite-t-elle jamais?

I am greatly indebted to Professor Mark Temmer of the University of California at Santa Barbara for this reference. Diderot is commenting on the French translation of the *Account* by Félicien Le Tourneur, 1771. Hill (see my note 5), III.434, n. 2, gives an excerpt from the critique, but does not identify it as by Diderot. Professor Temmer, in a work dealing with Johnson and *les philosophes*, still in progress, makes the interesting suggestion that Diderot's "neveu de Rameau," a pioneering "anti-hero," may to some extent be modelled on Savage.

22. Johnson, *Account*, pp. 38–39.
23. Tracy, *The Artificial Bastard*, pp. 6–7. Tracy here seems to indicate that the case against the truth of Savage's assertions *has* in fact been proven. If Lady Macclesfield was the kind of person described here, then Savage must have been lying about her vicious and pointless persecution of him. One cannot have it both ways.
24. See George Irwin, *Samuel Johnson: A Personality in Conflict* (Auckland, N. Z., 1971).
25. Johnson, *Account*, p. 43.
26. "Cet ouvrage eût été délicieux, et d'une finesse à comparer aux *Mémoires du Comte de Grammont*, si l'auteur anglais se fût proposé de faire la satire de son héros; mais malheureusement il est de bonne foi." See note 21.
27. Johnson, *Account*, p. 112.
28. Boswell, *Life of Johnson*, I.77.
29. Johnson, *Account*, p. 118.
30. Boswell, *Life of Johnson*, III.200.
31. Johnson, *Account*, p. 140, and n. 103.
32. What it is is advocacy, in the style later made popular by such famous defence counsel as Sir Edward Marshall Hall and Clarence Darrow. One thinks of Hall's peroration defending a woman accused of murder, "Look at her, gentlemen of the jury, look at her. God never gave her a chance. Won't you?" and Darrow's skilled use of then novel

psychiatric concepts in the defence of Leopold and Loeb. Johnson always had a hankering to be a lawyer. His skill as an advocate is perhaps shown to better advantage in his campaign to reprieve William Dodd in 1777.

33. See, e.g., Richard Schwartz, *Boswell's Johnson: A Preface to the Life* (Madison, 1978); Donald Greene, "Samuel Johnson," *The Craft of Literary Biography*, ed. Jeffrey Meyers (London, 1985), pp. 9–32, 233–240; *Boswell's Life of Johnson: New Questions, New Answers*, ed. John Vance (Athens, Georgia, 1985).

34. See note 21.

2   Boswell's *Life of Johnson*: *Maximillian E. Novak*

1. Germaine Greer, "Real Lives, or Readers' Digest?," *Times* (London), February 1, 1986, p. 8.
2. *Ibid.*
3. Although he is only indirectly concerned with literary biography, Philip Roth has made the relationship between the writer, his published work and his ensuing fame or infamy the subject of his most recent fiction, and in so doing, has expanded our understanding of the possibilities of this subject. The protagonist of Roth's trilogy, *Zuckerman Bound*, agrees to a degree with Greer on what seems to both of them an incorrect focus on biography rather than on an author's writings; but, inevitably, he also longs to have things both ways. He feels uncomfortable with his role as a celebrity, but enjoys some of the advantages of his notoriety. He wants to divorce himself from his writings in the same way that the New Critics attempted to separate the opinion of the author from any final judgment on the work of art, but he knows that, however transformed by his imagination, his fiction is ultimately drawn from his life experiences. However hard he tries to separate his life from his art, neither his family nor supposedly sophisticated critics will accept his explanations. Roth seems to see both the writer and audience in bad faith, and perhaps necessarily so. The reader wants to look beyond the work to create some form of biographical explanation; the writer tries to pretend that his work is somehow separate from himself. To bring these observations back to Greer's

complaint, it may be said that Boswell did not create the biographical curiosity about Johnson; he merely added to that inquisitiveness the ingredient of a curiosity about the biographer.

4. Thomas Babington Macaulay, "Boswell's *Life of Johnson,*" *Complete Works* (Boston, 1910), I.712. See also pp. 713–715, 731.

5. George F. Kennan, "History as Some Kind of Novel," *International Herald Tribune,* July 5–6, 1986.

6. Wayne Booth, *The Rhetoric of Fiction* (Chicago, 1961), especially pp. 67–86, 377–398.

7. Robert Darnton, *The Great Cat Massacre* (New York, 1985), pp. 215–256.

8. Robert Darnton, *Mesmerism* (New York, 1976), p. 117.

9. *Boswell on the Grand Tour,* ed. Frederick Pottle (New York, 1953), p. 200.

10. *Ibid.,* pp. 216–217.

11. The distinction is sketched out by Thomas Gray in his "Ode on a Distant Prospect of Eton College," in which he assumes that all men suffer pangs of sensibility, some in relationship with others and some in isolated egotism:

> To each his suff'rings: all are men
> Condemned alike to groan,
> The tender for another's pain;
> Th' unfeeling for his own. (ll. 91–94)

12. James Boswell, *Journal of a Tour to the Hebrides,* ed. R. W. Chapman (London, 1934), p. 192. Published with Samuel Johnson, *A Journey to the Western Islands.*

13. Quoted in G. B. Hill and L. F. Powell, eds., *Life of Johnson,* by James Boswell (Oxford, 1934), I.12–13.

14. Boswell, *Journal of a Tour,* p. 192.

15. *Boswell on the Grand Tour,* p. 44.

16. Boswell, *Journal of a Tour,* pp. 302–303. Boswell expanded this image considerably from his manuscript. Compare the manuscript version, *Journal of a Tour to the Hebrides,* ed. Frederick Pottle and Charles Bennett (London, 1936), p. 175.

17. Boswell, *Journal of a Tour,* p. 172.

18. James Boswell, *Life of Johnson,* ed. R. W. Chapman (London, 1953), p. 696.

19. Samuel Johnson, *The Rambler*, ed. W. J. Bate and Albrecht Strauss, in *Works* (New Haven, 1969), III.323.
20. Boswell, *Life*, pp. 20, 1327–1328.
21. Quoted in Hill and Powell, eds., *Life of Johnson*, I.12–13.
22. *How Does Analysis Cure?*, ed. Arnold Goldberg with Paul Stepansky (Chicago, 1984), pp. 17–22. Kohut argues that just as certain concepts seemed better suited for Freud's time, so, for our time, a philosophy of self might be the most useful focus. Frank Brady, Boswell's biographer, speaks of Boswell's feelings of castration in the presence of his father, but a "loss of self" might be a more accurate description for Boswell's period as well as our own.
23. Boswell, *Life of Johnson*, p. 331.
24. *Ibid.*, pp. 278–279.
25. *Ibid.*, p. 982.
26. *Ibid.*, p. 1235.
27. *Ibid.*, p. 25.
28. Quoted in Svetlana Alpers, *The Art of Describing* (Chicago, 1983), p. xxiii.
29. Sir Joshua Reynolds, *Discourses on Art*, ed. Robert Wark (San Marino, Calif., 1959), p. 124.
30. Boswell, *Life of Johnson*, p. 277.
31. *Ibid.*, pp. 280–281. For an excellent discussion of Boswell's adherence to a "Flemish" theory of detailed description in biography, see Frank Brady, *James Boswell: The Later Years 1769–1795* (London, 1984), p. 427. See also James Boswell, *The Ominous Years 1774–1776*, ed. Charles Ryscamp and Frederick Pottle (London, 1963), p. 103.
32. For a discussion of some of the complicated meanings of this word at the time, see my essay, "Gothic Fiction and the Grotesque," *Novel*, 13 (1979), 65–67.

3   Strachey's *Eminent Victorians*: Millicent Bell

1. "Lancaster Gate," *Lytton Strachey by Himself*, ed. Michael Holroyd (London, 1971), p. 26.
2. Lytton Strachey, "A Statesman: Lord Morley," *Characters and Commentaries* (London, 1933), pp. 215–216.
3. Strachey, "A Victorian Critic," *ibid.*, p. 175.

4. Lytton Strachey, "Preface," *Eminent Victorians* (New York and London, 1918), p. vii. Subsequent references to this edition will be indicated parenthetically.

5. Michael Holroyd, *Lytton Strachey*, 2 vols. (London, 1967–68), I.261–265 *passim*.

6. "Froude," *The Shorter Strachey*, ed. Michael Holroyd and Paul Levy (New York, 1980), p. 111. Originally titled "One of the Victorians," *Saturday Review of Literature*, 7 (December 6, 1930), 418–419; retitled "Froude," in *Portraits in Miniature and Other Essays* (London, 1931).

7. Edmund Sheridan Purcell, *Life of Cardinal Manning: Archbishop of Westminster*, 2 vols. (New York and London, 1896), I.xiii.

8. Sir Edward Cook, *The Life of Florence Nightingale*, 2 vols. (London, 1914), I.xxiv.

9. *Ibid.*, I.xxxi.

10. *Ibid.*, I.13–14.

11. F. A. Simpson, "Methods of History," *Spectator*, 172 (January 7, 1944), 7–8.

12. Purcell, *Manning*, I.416–417.

13. Cook, *Nightingale*, I.403.

14. Cecil Woodham-Smith, *Florence Nightingale* (London, 1950).

15. Cook, *Nightingale*, I.404.

16. Rosalind Nash, "Florence Nightingale According to Mr. Strachey," *Nineteenth Century*, 103 (February 1928), 263.

17. Holroyd, *Strachey*, I.280.

18. Edgar Johnson, *One Mighty Torrent* (New York, 1937), p. 53.

19. Purcell, *Manning*, I.85.

20. Arthur Penrhyn Stanley, *The Life and Correspondence of Thomas Arnold, D. D.* (Boston, 1862), 2 vols., I.114.

21. The episode is described in T. W. Banford's modern biography, *Thomas Arnold* (London, 1960), pp. 49–53.

22. F. B. Smith, *Florence Nightingale: Reputation and Power* (London, 1982).

23. Smith, *Nightingale*, p. 52.

24. Cook, *Nightingale*, I.100–101.

25. Smith, *Nightingale*, p. 37.

26. Cook, *Nightingale*, I.xxvi.

27. Holroyd, *Strachey*, I.404.

4 Symons' *The Quest for Corvo*: A. O. J. Cockshut

1. Osbert Sitwell, *The Scarlet Tree* (London, 1946), p. 257.
2. *Ibid.*
3. See my book, *Truth to Life* (London, 1974), for a detailed discussion of this type of biography.
4. See Donald Weeks, *Corvo* (London, 1971) and Miriam Benkovitz, *Frederick Rolfe: Baron Corvo* (London, 1977).
5. A. J. A. Symons, *Essays and Biographies*, ed. Julian Symons (London, 1969), p. 11.
6. *Ibid.*
7. See Julian Symons, *A. J. A. Symons: His Life and Speculations* (London, 1950), *passim*.
8. A. J. A. Symons, *Essays and Biographies*, pp. 79–80.
9. Julian Symons, *A. J. A. Symons*, p. 5.
10. *Ibid.*, p. 109.
11. *Ibid.*, p. 33.
12. *Ibid.*, p. 214.
13. *Ibid.*, p. 55.
14. *Ibid.*, p. 272.
15. *Ibid.*, p. 203.
16. A. J. A. Symons, *Essays and Biographies*, p. 7.
17. *Ibid.*, p. 6.
18. A. J. A. Symons, *The Quest for Corvo: An Experiment in Biography*, with an Introduction by Julian Symons (London, 1955), p. 5.
19. *Ibid.*, p. 10.
20. *Ibid.*, p. 79.
21. *Ibid.*, p. 222.
22. *Ibid.*, p. 48.
23. *Ibid.*, p. 59.
24. *Ibid.*, p. 65.
25. *Ibid.*, pp. 65–66.
26. *Ibid.*, p. 79.
27. *Ibid.*, p. 110n.
28. *Ibid.*, p. 162.
29. Sitwell, *The Scarlet Tree*, p. 259.
30. A. J. A. Symons, *The Quest for Corvo*, p. 84.
31. *Ibid.*, p. 142.
32. *Ibid.*, pp. 120–125.
33. *Ibid.*, pp. 137–138.
34. *Ibid.*, p. 223.

35. *Ibid.*
36. A. J. A. Symons, *The Quest for Corvo*, p. 205.
37. Weeks, *Corvo*, pp. 304ff.
38. Graham Greene, "Frederick Rolfe: Edwardian Inferno," *The Lost Childhood* (London, 1951), pp. 92–93.
39. *Ibid.*, p. 94.
40. *Ibid.*, pp. 94–95.
41. A. J. A. Symons, *Essays and Biographies*, pp. 145–190.
42. Weeks, *Corvo*, p. 244.
43. *Ibid.*, p. 334.
44. A. J. A. Symons, *The Quest for Corvo*, p. 79.
45. D. H. Lawrence, "*Hadrian the Seventh*, by Baron Corvo," *Phoenix*, ed. Edward McDonald (London, 1936), p. 329.
46. *Ibid.*, p. 327.
47. From a typed transcript of a letter, afterwards destroyed; in the possession of Mrs. Julia Briggs.
48. Weeks, *Corvo*, pp. 333–334.
49. From a typed transcript of a letter, afterwards destroyed; in the possession of Mrs. Julia Briggs.
50. Rolfe's letter to Rev. J. S. Serjeant, quoted in Weeks, *Corvo*, pp. 358–359.
51. J. C. Powys, *Autobiography* (London, 1967), p. 411.

5 Ellmann's *James Joyce*: Phillip F. Herring

1. Henry James, *The Turn of the Screw and Other Short Novels* (New York, 1962), p. 233.
2. James Joyce, *Finnegans Wake* (New York, 1939), p. 55:06.
3. Germaine Greer, "Real Lives, or Readers' Digest?," *Times* (London), February 1, 1986, p. 8.
4. Herbert Gorman, *James Joyce* (New York, 1939).
5. References to the two editions of Ellmann's biography *James Joyce* (New York, 1959; 1982) are cited in my text as *JJ1* and *JJ2*.
6. Richard Ellmann, "Freud and Literary Biography," *American Scholar*, 53 (Autumn 1984), 472.
7. *Ibid.*, pp. 476–477.
8. Richard Ellmann, *Golden Codgers* (London, 1973), p. 9.
9. *Ibid.*, p. 15.
10. *Ibid.*, pp. 2–3.

11. Richard Ellmann, *James Joyce's Hundredth Birthday: Side and Front Views* (Washington, D.C., 1982), p. 24.
12. Robert Adams, "In Joyce's Wake," *Hudson Review*, 12 (Winter 1959–60), 627.
13. Katherine Frank, "Writing Lives: Theory and Practice in Literary Biography," *Genre*, 13 (Winter 1980), 502.
14. David Greene, "Joyce: Portrait Without Irony," *Nation*, 189 (October 17, 1959), 234.
15. Horace Reynolds, "The Complex Joyce in Ellmann Biography," *Christian Science Monitor*, October 22, 1959, p. 11.
16. Kristian Smidt, *English Studies*, 41 (October 1960), 337.
17. Hugh Kenner, *Times Literary Supplement*, December 17, 1982, p. 1383.
18. J. B. Bamborough, *Review of English Studies*, 12 (February 1961), 105.
19. Christopher Ricks, *Grand Street*, 2 (Spring 1983), 88.
20. Chester Anderson, *Irish Literary Supplement*, 2, ii (1983), 13.
21. Joseph Prescott, *Modern Philology*, 58 (November 1960), 148.
22. Arnold Goldman, " 'Now' in the 'Post-Now' Era," *James Joyce Broadsheet*, 10 (February 1983), 1.
23. Kenner, *TLS*, p. 1383. The disagreement, even hostility, between Ellmann and Kenner on this issue has been much commented upon privately. One origin may be what seems to be a mean-spirited book review by Ellmann of Clive Hart and David Hayman, eds., *James Joyce's ULYSSES: Critical Essays*, which appeared in *TLS* on October 3, 1975, where Kenner perhaps received more than his share of criticism. Ellmann took aim at him again in his review "The New *Ulysses*," which post-dated Kenner's *TLS* review of the revised biography of Joyce, for which review, Ellmann writes me, the editor of *TLS* apologized.
24. *Ibid.*, p. 1384.
25. James Joyce, *Ulysses* (Harmondsworth, Middlesex, 1969), pp. 707–708.
26. Ellmann checked O'Nolan's story with Niall Sheridan, Niall Montgomery, John Garvin, O'Nolan's wife and brother. None apparently believed O'Nolan's claim to have authored the John Joyce interview, and to family members no such claim was made. (Letter to me of August 27, 1986 from Richard Ellmann.)

27. Kenner, *TLS*, p. 1384.
28. William Noon, S. J., "A Delayed Review, *James Joyce* by Richard Ellmann," *James Joyce Quarterly*, 2 (Fall 1964), 7–12.
29. Robert Scholes, *James Joyce Quarterly*, 2 (Summer 1965), 310–313; Ruth von Phul, *James Joyce Quarterly*, 3 (Fall 1965), 69–72.
30. Niall Montgomery, *Studies* (Dublin), 49 (Summer 1960), 208.
31. Phillip F. Herring, "Joyce's Politics," *New Light on Joyce from the Dublin Symposium*, ed. Fritz Senn (Bloomington, Indiana, 1972), pp. 3–14.
32. *The Letters of James Joyce*, eds. Stuart Gilbert (vol. I) and Richard Ellmann (vols. II and III) (New York, 1957–66). Hereafter referred to as the *Letters*.
33. James Joyce, *A Portrait of the Artist as a Young Man* (New York, 1964), p. 253.
34. Guglielmo Ferrero, *L'Europa giovane* (Milan, 1897), p. 366; Robert Scholes, "x/y: Joyce and Modernist Ideology," unpublished paper, 1986, p. 14.
35. The same could be said for Manganiello, whose book was the first to define carefully Joyce's politics and make us generally aware of Ferrero. It has laid the groundwork for further investigation in this area.
36. William Empson, *Using Biography* (Cambridge, Mass., 1984), p. 219; Hugh Kenner, *Dublin's Joyce* (Boston, 1962). In his *New Statesmen* review, 58 (October 31, 1959), 585–586), Empson objected to Ellmann's description of Joyce's politics in the biography.
37. Richard Ellmann, *The Consciousness of Joyce* (New York, 1977).
38. Richard Ellmann, "Joyce and Politics," *Joyce and Paris*, ed. Jacques Aubert and Maria Jolas (Paris, 1979), p. 31.
39. *Ibid.*
40. "Ellmann Rejoicing," *New York Times Book Review*, September 19, 1982, pp. 7, 24.
41. See Kimberly Devlin, "The Romance Heroine Exposed: 'Nausicaa and *The Lamplighter*,' " *James Joyce Quarterly*, 22 (Summer 1985), 383–396.
42. Bernard McCabe makes this point in the *Nation*, 235 (November 20, 1982), 528.

43. Charles Peake, "The Depths of Impersonality," *Times Higher Education Supplement*, December 31, 1982, p. 8.
44. Philip Gaskell, *Essays in Criticism*, 33 (July 1983), 253.
45. Smidt, *English Studies*, p. 336.
46. *Times Literary Supplement*, November 20, 1959, p. 669.
47. *The James Joyce Archive*, ed. Michael Groden *et al.*, 63 vols. (New York, 1978).
48. *Joyce and Hauptmann*, ed. Jill Perkins (Pasadena, California, 1978).
49. *The Letters of James Joyce*, ed. Stuart Gilbert (New York, 1957).
50. *Selected Letters of James Joyce*, ed. Richard Ellmann (New York, 1975).
51. Denis Donoghue, *London Review of Books*, September 20–October 3, 1984, p. 15. Ellmann, *Golden Codgers*, pp. 2–3.
52. James Joyce, *Giacomo Joyce*, ed. Richard Ellmann (New York, 1968).
53. Horace Reynolds, *Christian Science Monitor*, p. 11.
54. *The Critical Writings of James Joyce*, ed. Ellsworth Mason and Richard Ellmann (New York, 1959), p. 273, quoted in Stephen Spender, "All Life Was Grist for the Artist," *New York Times Book Review*, October 25, 1959, p. 58.

6 Painter's *Marcel Proust*: *Jeffrey Meyers*

1. *World Authors, 1950–1970* (New York, 1975), pp. 1107–1108.
2. Lewis Nichols, "Double Toil," *New York Times Book Review*, November 7, 1965, p. 8.
3. Phyllis Grosskurth, "An Interview with George Painter," *Salmagundi*, 6 (1983), 26.
4. Letter from George Painter to Jeffrey Meyers, January 13–28, 1986.
5. *World Authors*, p. 1108.
6. *Ibid.*
7. Letter from Painter to Meyers.
8. Simon Blow, "A stake in the past," *Guardian*, October 19, 1977, p. 10.
9. Grosskurth, *Salmagundi*, p. 36. For more information on Painter, see *Contemporary Authors*, vol. 101 (Detroit, 1981), pp. 359–360, and *Who's Who* (London, 1985), p. 1466.

10. George Painter, *André Gide: A Critical and Biographical Study* (New York, 1951), p. 7.
11. Marcel Proust, *Remembrance of Things Past*, trans. C. K. Scott-Moncrieff (New York, 1934), II.130.
12. Letter from Painter to Meyers.
13. Grosskurth, *Salmagundi*, pp. 40–41.
14. *Ibid.*, p. 35.
15. Blow, *Guardian*, p. 10.
16. Grosskurth, *Salmagundi*, pp. 37–38. The first volume of *Chateaubriand* was dedicated, in part, to Marthe Bibesco.
17. *Ibid.*, pp. 39–40.
18. *Ibid.*, p. 28. It is worth noting that Painter's Foreword to *William Caxton: A Biography* (London, 1976), p. vii, remains unregenerate and asserts, like his Preface to *Marcel Proust*, that the sources for his life "have not as yet been adequately studied or interpreted"; that the biography is based on "an independent study of the primary sources"; that it is written "for the general reader, the student, and the specialist alike"; and that there are many new facts and new conclusions.
19. Letter from Painter to Meyers.
20. George Painter, *Marcel Proust: A Biography* (London, 1959), I.xi–xii.
21. *World Authors*, p. 1108.
22. Grosskurth, *Salmagundi*, p. 37, relates that in *Other People's Letters* Mina Curtiss "talks about the period when she went to Paris to collect Proust's letters and how she went to bed with the Prince Bibesco in order to obtain letters." Painter wrote a favorable review of Curtiss' edition in the *Listener*, 44 (December 21, 1950), 801. For Painter's reviews of books on Proust by Harold March and F. C. Green, see *Listener*, 41 (May 19, 1949), 861–862 and 42 (December 8, 1949), 1009, 1011.
23. Grosskurth, *Salmagundi*, p. 26.
24. See Marie Riefstahl-Nordlinger, "On Reading *Marcel Proust—A Biography*, Vol. 1, by George D. Painter," *X, A Quarterly Review*, 1 (July 1960), 203–209, and "A Reply to Mme. Riefstahl-Nordlinger from George D. Painter," *X, A Quarterly Review*, 1 (October 1960), 322–324.
25. George Painter, "Proust's Way," *Times Literary Supplement*, August 19, 1965, p. 715. See also Painter, "Proust's Way," *Times Literary Supplement*, September 9, 1965, p. 775.

26. Grosskurth, *Salmagundi*, p. 33.
27. This sentence and many others appear in "Proust's Way," Painter's Introduction to Proust's *Letters to His Mother* (London, 1956), pp. 32–48. In this essay, he presents a concise life of Proust and emphasizes the originals of his fictional characters.

7 Edel's *Henry James*: *Eugene Goodheart*

1. T. S. Eliot, "Tradition and the Individual Talent" (1919), *Selected Essays, 1917–1932* (New York, 1932), p. 11.
2. Quoted in Leon Edel, "The Figure Under the Carpet," *Telling Lives*, ed. Marc Pachter (Washington, D.C., 1979), p. 21.
3. Leon Edel, *Literary Biography* (Toronto, 1957), p. 125.
4. A word I normally do not like to employ. But Edel's performance requires a characterization stronger than sympathy.
5. Leon Edel, *Henry James: The Untried Years (1843—1870)* (Philadelphia, 1953), p. 14.
6. Henry James, *Autobiography*, ed. Frederick W. Dupee (Princeton, 1983), pp. 414–415.
7. *Ibid.*, p. 457.
8. Leon Edel, *Henry James: The Treacherous Years (1895–1901)* (Philadelphia, 1969), p. 212.
9. *Ibid.*, p. 17.
10. See *Ibid.*, pp. 66, 72.
11. *Ibid.*, p. 58.
12. See Leon Edel, "The Figure Under the Carpet."
13. Leon Edel, *Henry James: The Master (1901–1916)* (Philadelphia, 1972), p. 162.
14. Quentin Anderson, "Leon Edel's *Henry James*," *Virginia Quarterly Review*, 48 (Fall 1972), 623–624.
15. Leon Edel, "Biography and the Narrator," *New Republic*, 152 (March 6, 1965), 25.
16. Quentin Anderson, "Leon Edel's *Henry James*," pp. 623–624.
17. Leon Edel, *Henry James: The Conquest of London (1870–1881)* (Philadelphia, 1962), p. 276.

18. Millicent Bell, "Henry James: The Man Who Lived," *Massachusetts Review*, 14 (Spring 1973), 403.
19. Edel, *The Conquest of London*, p. 255.
20. Edel, *The Master*, p. 536.
21. Mark Krupnick, "Henry James: The Artist as Emperor," *Novel*, 6 (Spring 1973), 258.
22. *Ibid.*, p. 259.
23. *Ibid.*
24. Edel, *The Treacherous Years*, p. 350.
25. Edel, *The Conquest of London*, p. 428.
26. Edel, *The Master*, p. 110.
27. *Ibid.*, p. 112.
28. *Ibid.*, p. 114.
29. *Ibid.*, p. 116.
30. *Ibid.*, p. 119.
31. *Ibid.*, p. 122.
32. Leon Edel, *The Middle Years (1882–1895)* (Philadelphia, 1962), p. 214.
33. *Ibid.*, p. 334.
34. Edel, *The Treacherous Years*, p. 113.
35. *Ibid.*, p. 407.
36. *Ibid.*, p. 474.
37. *Ibid.*, p. 473.

Index

I. BIOGRAPHY

Biographer:
  attitude to subject, 1–4, 7, 23–24, 37–
    38, 41–43, 45, 53–55, 60–71, 73,
    74, 77–79, 82, 85, 89–90, 91, 106,
    116, 130, 133–134, 148, 150, 152–
    153, 159, 160, 165
  requirements of, 5–6, 107, 142, 148,
    151
  self-projection, 6, 7, 26–28, 86–87
Literary Biography:
  aims: didactic, 17, 59–60, 67;
    exploration of creative process,
    131, 136, 140, 142, 148, 149–150;
    hagiography, 77–78; memorialize,
    57
  art of: biographical license, 108, 113,
    115, 133, 134, 165; detection, 1, 2,
    5, 8, 52, 88, 95, 129, 139, 150–151,
    153; fictionalizing, 30, 61;
    narrative, 7, 8, 9, 57; novelistic,
    151, 155, 156, 162, 165; period
    atmosphere, 88, 132; point of view,
    38, 56, 86, 96, 161–162
  attacks on, 2–4, 32–33, 106, 149, 150,
    173 n3
  criticism of, 6
  gossip, 32–33
  intimate details, 141
  objectivity, 37–38
  psychoanalytic, 9, 91, 107, 155–156,
    159, 163
  psychological, 16–17, 86
  speculation, 8, 88, 108
  truth in, 2, 7, 8, 9, 43, 55–56, 113, 125–
    126, 151, 155
  types of: brief lives, 59; definitions, 129,
    132, 151; prefatory lives, 14–15;
    text-based, 131
  value of criticism, 136, 137, 140–141,
    149–150, 166
  Victorian model, 85–86, 87

II. NAMES

Adams, Henry, 157; *The Education of Henry
  Adams*, 2
Adams, Robert, 112
Adler, Alfred, 91, 154
Anastasia, Grand Duchess, 20, 21
Anderson, Chester, 114
Anderson, Hendrik, 9, 163, 165
Anderson, Quentin, 157, 158, 166
Arnold, Matthew, 54; "Rugby Chapel,"
  65
Arnold, Thomas, 55, 64, 66, 69–71, 77,
  81–82, 83
Ascham, Roger, 13
Aubrey, John, 59
Auden, W. H., 4; *Letters from Iceland*, 5;
  "Who's Who," 5

Bair, Deirdre, *Samuel Beckett*, 123
Bakhtin, Mikhail, 38
Balzac, Honoré de, 154, 163, 165
Bamborough, J. B., 114
Banford, T. W., *Thomas Arnold*, 176
  n21
Bangs, John Kendrick, 35, 42; *The
  Houseboat on the Styx*, 31; *The Pursuit
  of the Houseboat*, 31
Baring, Sir Evelyn, 65, 76, 77
Barker, Richard, 138–139, 141
Barretier, Jean-Philippe, 13
Bate, Walter Jackson, 31–32
Beach, Sylvia, 111
Beardsley, Aubrey, 92
Beckett, Samuel, 123
Bell, Millicent, viii, 7, 53–83, 158
Benson, Robert Hugh, 96–97
Bentley, Edmund, 5
Bibesco, Marthe, 133
Birkenhead, Earl, *Rudyard Kipling*,
  3
Birrell, Augustine, 63
Blow, Simon, 131, 134